D1438034

The City Silent

Robert J. Smith

Published by
Douglas McLean
8 St. John Street
Coleford
Gloucestershire GL16 8AR
England
www.ForestBooks.com

ISBN 0 946252 52 1

Printed in Great Britain by
CopyPlus: Tel: 01600 772600

CONTENTS

Dedication

Acknowledgements

Author's Note

Foreword

Introduction by Gordon M Chapman

DEDICATION

For my father and brother, Tom and Kenny; affectionately remembered.

FOREWORD

In writing and compiling this book, my main objective is to tell the story of Deaf Connections; outlining its History and Development, but in doing so, I seek to increase the awareness of the reader, Deaf or Hearing, as to the condition, past and present, of the Deaf in our society, and how that may change in the future.

AUTHOR'S NOTE

Name of the Society

Deaf Connections, throughout its History, has been bedevilled by public confusion over its name and role. Name changes have been relatively frequent, so some of the confusion may be partially self inflicted, but most of the changes have been forced on the Society due to changing social circumstances, and the need to maintain its own distinct identity. In the interests of clarity, I will refer to Deaf Connections throughout as *'The Society'*, except when direct quotes are used.

An outline of the evolution of the Society's name appears in Appendix i.

ACKNOWLEDGEMENTS

Sincere thanks to all at Deaf Connections for their invaluable assistance. Special thanks to Liz McKinney for recommending me, to Gordon Chapman for sparing me so much of his valuable time, to Gillian Nixon for giving me a copy of her thesis, to Cathie for 'finding me a home' to May for her superb typing skills, to Tracy for her I.T. wizardry and to Doug McLean of Forest Books and Peter King of CopyPlus for their invaluable assistance. Finally thanks to Joanne, Rowan and Lewis for their encouragement and tolerance.

EPHPHATHA

There is a Living Realm where Silence reigns,
Mute as the Dead are in their lonesome halls
Where lowing herds are heard not in the plains
And on the hills are voiceless waterfalls.

No song salutes the morning at her gates,
From soaring lark or linnet in the vale;
On drowsy noon no droning creature waits,
Eve has no thrush, and night no nightingale.

The sea is heard, the thunder-riven sky,
The groaning forest when the tempest swells,
As in a dream one hears an angel sigh
Or hears the twinkling of heather bells.

The city silent, with all its rushing wheels,
And tread of myriads hurrying to and fro,
As when thro' haunted house a phantom steals-
All silent as the sound of falling snow.'

THOMAS DUNLOP (EXCERPT)
(WRITTEN SPECIALLY FOR THE 1883 REPORT)

'I do not think there is any section of the Disabled in the Community that has been more imposed on than the Deaf. I do not know any affliction that is more difficult to bear. As I see it, at any rate, Deafness has in it the possibilities of more disturbance than any of the other common Disabilities.'

MR TOMLINSON
(CHIEF ARCHITECT OF THE DISABLED PERSON
[EMPLOYMENT] ACT 1944)

'I find Deafness my greatest handicap'
'Blindness cuts you off from Things, but deafness cuts you off from People'

HELEN KELLER

'There stands opposed to the true history of my people, whose modern era began when the Abbe de L'Epee discovered how to educate us through Sign Language, quite another History. It is a record of the efforts of Hearing people to supplant the Language of the Deaf with their Language, to replace signs with speech. It calls itself the History of the Deaf - yet it is an account not of my people but of our Hearing Benefactors, who affirm that the only proper route for elevating the Deaf is Oral Instruction. It is a False History.'

HARLAN LANE
(EXCERPT FROM 'WHEN THE MIND HEARS')

INTRODUCTION

Deaf Connections is one of the oldest organisations for Adult Deaf people in this country, and indeed in the World. We are very proud of this. I am frequently asked just how long we've been going for. When I answer that the Society was established in 1822, many people shrug their shoulders, having no concept of just how long ago that was. Then when I state that this was not long after the Battle of Waterloo, their surprise is often palpable. They, like many others, imagine that organisations for the welfare of Deaf people are relatively recent phenomena, products of the Welfare State.

We in Deaf Connections owe a huge debt to the visionary individuals; Deaf and Hearing, who nurtured the Society through its difficult early days until it blossomed into one of the foremost organisations for Deaf people in the country. Throughout this book you will find key figures: the Movers and Shakers of their day, who influenced the shape and form of the Society.

In my position as Chief Executive, I am conscious that I am 'Standing on the shoulders of Giants': John Henderson, William Agnew, Stanley Craig, Stewart Lochrie and others. Sometimes I wish I could go back in time to meet them, or even ask their advice.

Within the book, you will see recurring examples of the inherent tension between the Deaf members and the mainly Hearing Board of Directors. This tension has sometimes been a creative force as well as a negative one, but now that we are moving towards a more Egalitarian Society, positive steps have been taken to ensure that Deaf people play a major part in the decision making process. This journey has just started, and it may be a long one, but one well worth making.

Times have changed, but some things remain constant. Throughout our history, we in the Society have had to adapt to meet the needs of Deaf people in response to the changing nature of Society as a whole. This adaptability has been the key to our success. Now that we have entered the new Millennium this is as true as ever.

My grateful thanks to Robert for his sterling work in negotiating his way through the morass of our Archives in order to tell our story. Thanks also to all others who helped bring the book to fruition.

It is my hope that readers of 'The City Silent' will learn not just about our organisation, but about the condition and culture of Deaf people in the West of Scotland, which will probably be mirrored throughout the country as a whole.

Gordon M. Chapman, Chief Executive, February 2001

CHAPTER 1

'TO BEAR PATIENTLY THEIR DAILY BURDEN'

-❀- OUR DESIGN. ❀-

❉ ❉ ❉

TO carry the Gospel to the **DEAF** and **DUMB** of this great City, and throughout the towns of the West of Scotland; to help them to bear patiently their daily burden, and to resist firmly all evil and intemperate habits; to raise the standard of right among them; and, with the Divine blessing, to lead them to a knowledge of Him who "hath done all things well, who maketh both the deaf to hear and the dumb to speak."

In the Annual Report of 1876, the Missionary of the Glasgow Mission to the Deaf and Dumb, A. Frederick Woodbridge, writes seeking to clarify the aims and objectives of the Society, necessary due to the prevailing confusion over its role. *'As many persons seem to mistake the Design of the Society, permit me to explain in this place that it is not an Institution of the Education of the Young, but a special Mission to those who, having completed their curriculum at the Deaf and Dumb Institution, have been discharged from its sheltering walls, and are now thrown upon their own resources, and exposed to all the Temptations of Life. Our object is to meet them at this point - to be a friend and pastor to them in every time of need - to carry on their Education to a higher point - viz to a knowledge of Christ; and thus to fit them for filling with honour the positions they occupy here, and to prepare them for the great 'Hereafter'.*

1

It may be asked, is all this necessary? The children have completed their five or six years' course of training in the Institution, are they not now fitted for the Battle of Life. The answer is a plain and distinct one. They have left the only place where they could understand and be understood, and have now to mix with their fellow creatures to earn their livelihood, from the greater part of whom they are still separated by the impassable barrier of non-communication. The parents being desirous, perhaps, of keeping up the good habits formed at school, take them to their own church, where the services are conducted orally. The child cannot comprehend the prayers or sermon because he cannot hear, and the consequence is a dislike to attend church, which so increases upon him that as soon as he is free of parental restraint, he absents himself altogether. The necessity of providing some remedy is therefore apparent to all who have the interest of the Deaf and Dumb at heart.

In order to meet this want, our Mission has established Sabbath Services, weekly Prayer Meetings, Lectures, Bible Class etc in the finger and sign language - a language understood by the people; and the amount of good, which has attended these efforts for our isolated brethren, testified plainly to their importance, and must be exceedingly gratifying to you as Directors of this work and to all who have assisted in it.

The light in which the Deaf and Dumb of other towns, who are not so fortunately placed, regard it, is clear evidence of its usefulness and worth.

One writes: 'I am desirous to let you know that with the view of receiving a greater amount of spiritual good than Greenock can produce, I have been long-ing to be settled in Glasgow, in which I spent the happy days of my boyhood.' And many are the wishes expressed by numerous correspondents to reside here, in order to enjoy the advantages which this society affords.'

Since Frederick Woodbridge was the Missionary, it is perhaps not surprising that he should put particular emphasis on the religious dimension in his eloquent synopsis. The 'Our Design' Mission Statement, however, also makes it clear that this was also the case for the Society in general.

But even in Victorian times, the Social and Educational objectives of the Society were also important, as an excerpt from the summary of work of the Missionary for 1880 reveals: -

BAPTISMS - 3, MARRIAGES - 2, FUNERAL SERVICES - 9,

COURT CASES INTERPRETED - 5, MEMBERS VISITED - 232.

SITUATIONS SECURED FOR: - MEN - 28, WOMEN - 11, BOYS - 4, GIRLS - 1.

The programme of Lectures for 1879 also stresses the Educational objectives to the Adult Deaf of the Society.

The above, then, may give a more rounded picture of the work of the Society at that time; though doubtless Woodbridge would have given primacy to 'saving souls' over all other objectives.

What then were the Origins of the Society?

The Society; the first such organisation for the Adult Deaf in the Country, was instituted in Glasgow in 1822.

Its roots, however, can be traced to the first School for the Education of the Deaf in Britain, founded by Thomas Braidwood in Edinburgh in the 1760's, around the same time as L'Abbe de L'Epee began teaching the Deaf in France. This School was known as Braidwood's Academy, or with the typical sensitivity of the Hearing towards the Deaf, as Dumbiedykes. It was situated at Craigside House, on St Leonard's Hill near Holyrood Palace.

Dr Samuel Johnston visited the School in 1773 in the course of his travels to the Western Isles:-

'There is one subject of Philosophical Curiosity in Edinburgh, which no other city has to show; a College of the Deaf, who are taught to speak, to read, and to write and to practise arithmetic, by a gentleman whose name is Braidwood. It was pleasing to see one of the most desperate of human calamities capable of so much help: whatever enlarges hope will exalt courage. After having seen the Deaf taught arithmetic, who would be afraid to cultivate the Hebrides?'

Another visitor to Braidwood's Academy, less famous but more important to the Deaf, was Thomas Gallaudet, the Father of the American Deaf, who sought in 1815 to learn instruction in the signing used to educate the children from the Head Teacher, Robert Kinniburgh . This plea, on instructions from Thomas Braidwood, the grandson of the founder already mentioned, was refused, forcing Gallaudet to voyage instead to Paris for instruction from L'Abbe Sicard, a pupil of L'Epee, the founder of the first School for the Deaf, and so paving the way for the adoption of the European single system of signing in American sign language.

It was from Braidwood's Academy that in 1814, one year previously, Mr Kinniburgh visited Glasgow with some of his pupils, demonstrating what could be achieved in the Education of the Deaf.

Due to the stimulus provided by this visit, an Auxiliary Society of the Edinburgh School was instituted in Glasgow, which set up a small school for the Education of the Deaf at 38 High John Street shortly after. Mr John Anderson was appointed as the first ever Teacher of the Deaf in Glasgow.

However, it is evident that Glasgow/Edinburgh rivalry flourished in the 19th century as in the present day, since in 1818, a section of the Great and Good, and those interested in the Education of the Deaf issued a pamphlet signed by leading citizens stressing the desirability of the foundation of an independent Institution in Glasgow. Whatever Edinburgh could do, Glasgow could do just as well: if not better, thank you very much.

As a consequence of this, a Public Meeting was held on the 14th of January 1819 in the Andersonian Institution Room with the then Lord Provost Henry Monteith presiding.

Some of the 22 children attending the school were examined and an Educational Report, compiled by John Anderson, was read, concluding in a statement stressing the necessity of expanding the provision for the Education of Deaf children in Glasgow.

The Lord Provost, pleased by what he had witnessed, moved that, *'The Meeting is deeply impressed with the importance and the necessity of Institutions for the Education of the Deaf and Dumb, and therefore a Society be immediately formed in this City, the Design of which shall be to provide gratuitously the means of instruction for the children of those who are indigent, and, at certain rates according to their circumstances, for those who are able to pay for it.'* Note the echo of current funding philosophy. The resolution was passed without opposition.

Consequently a Society called 'The Glasgow Society for the Education of the Deaf and Dumb' was formed with the Lord Provost as President, Andrew Tennent as Treasurer, and the Rev Dr William Muir as Secretary. Within a very short time a sum of just under £2,000 was raised.

Land for a house and schoolroom was quickly purchased at Barony Glebe: *'A situation at once retired, well aired and not too distant from the town.'*

The Foundation Stone of this first school (whose address became 38 Parson Street) was laid in March 1820. John Anderson was invited to become Headmaster. By April 1821, the school had 50 pupils with 2 additional teachers.

4

Barony Glebe School, the first school for the deaf in Glasgow

However, in spite of this promising beginning, problems rapidly began to fester behind the scenes. Due to a *'Misunderstanding'* between himself and the Directors, John Anderson resigned from his post in 1822.

'Misunderstanding' was clearly a euphemism for 'Major bust up'; illustrated by the fact that Anderson immediately opened a Private School for the Deaf at St Andrew's Square, taking many of his former pupils with him.

The Archives do not reveal the root cause of Anderson's resignation, but it may be implied that it was over salary and general financial arrangements for the running of the School, or, perhaps more likely, disagreements over educational policy and philosophy.

At any rate, this was the crucial catalyst for the Foundation of the Society. It is abundantly clear that Anderson took a very modern, holistic view of Education, and this combined with, it can be implied, strong religious convictions, caused him to establish Prayer Meetings for young deaf people who had left formal education. These meetings, held in his own house in St Andrew's Square, were initially attended by some 10 young deaf men and women. Perhaps it was this concern for the welfare of the adult deaf which was partly responsible for Anderson's resignation.

Whatever the truth of the matter, the commencement of Anderson's Prayer Meetings can be seen as the genesis of the Society: initially termed 'The Scottish Association for the Deaf and Dumb, Glasgow Branch', an organisation primarily focused on the needs of the Adult Deaf. No portrait of John Anderson survives, but one can gain a strong impression of his character from his next action. Having successfully established a Private School for the Deaf in

5

Glasgow, and instituted the Society in the form of Prayer Meetings; after only 2 years he left Glasgow for Liverpool in 1824, in order to found an Institution for the Deaf.

Anderson gives the impression of being a driven, mercurial individual imbued with Missionary zeal. The quiet life did not seem to be for him.

The Barony Glebe School continued in a weakened state until it was stabilized under the Headship of Duncan Anderson, Head from 1831 until 1869. However, the Private School founded by John Anderson at St Andrew's Square seems to have been disbanded. The Society, in the form of Prayer Meetings, continued, albeit in a sickly form, under the Leadership of Mr J Ferguson. Meetings were held every Sunday afternoon in a medical lecture room in North Portland Street with an average attendance of between 15 and 20, but this state of affairs lasted for only a year, due to the departure of Ferguson on his Ordination as a Minister of the Church of England.

The former pupils of both schools were now left to their own resources. Irregular meetings and services were held and conducted by members of the Society themselves for many years.

At last in 1844, deeply dissatisfied with the situation, members convened a Meeting, at which it was decided to seek the assistance of the Barony Glebe School. They chose as their representative Mr William Ure, a long serving member, whose task it was to solicit the aid of the longstanding Headmaster Duncan Anderson. After meeting Mr Anderson and the School Secretary Mr Penney, it was decided to hire a hall at the Andersonian University for services. Mr Ure volunteered to conduct these meetings.

Around 25 members attended regularly and Ure continued his work for 3 years until his retiral due to ill health.

Archibald Cameron continued the work; now in Balfour's School, North Portland Street, for 2 years until, *'His mind became affected, and he was sent to Gartnavel Lunatic Asylum.'*

Meetings continued in an irregular form for the next few years as follows:-

YEAR	LEADER	PLACE
1854-56	COLIN CAMPBELL	ANDERSONIAN UNIVERSITY
1857-59	WILLIAM CURLE	Y.M.C.A, N. FREDERICK STREET
1864-68	DANIEL WEIR	ANDERSONIAN UNIVERSITY
1868-70	JOHN WEIR	ANDERSONIAN UNIVERSITY

By the time of the death of John Weir in 1870, the Society had reached crisis point; the funds being only 4s 7d. There was great concern amongst members that its demise was imminent.

As a stop gap measure, David Lindsay, John Heggie and James Paul volunteered to take charge of services in turns, until this task was taken on by Alex Strathern from the end of 1870 until 1873.

In order to place the Society on a firmer footing, it was resolved to form a Committee of Management. This was achieved with the aid of several of the Directors of the Institution for the Education of Deaf Children, which had been since 1868 sited at Langside (it is now Langside College).

The Committee produced the first ever Annual Report for the years 1871 - 1872. Due to the enthusiasm of the new Committee, a healthier balance of £13/11s/9d, mainly derived from collections, was able to be transferred to the next financial year, with the following sentiment:- *'Thanks however, be to God, these clouds have been dispelled, and your Committee have now to render him praise for putting it into the hearts of his people to contribute more liberally to this Society's funds during the past year than they had ever done before.'*

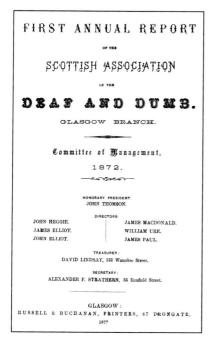

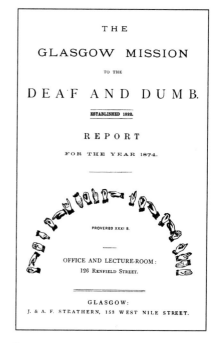

First ever Annual Report produced by the Society; 1871-2

First Glasgow Mission Report 1874. The text from proverbs 31 v8 (Authorised Version) reads, 'Open thy mouth for the dumb.' A modern translation would read, 'Speak up for those who cannot help themselves'

7

At a general meeting in Whyte's Temperance Hotel in Candleriggs on 11th October 1872 with Alex Strathern in the chair, it was proposed that the Scottish Deaf and Dumb Association (Glasgow Branch) should cease to exist and that a new Association be formed forthwith.

After some debate, it was decided on 18th October that the new Association be termed 'The Glasgow Christian Association of Deaf and Dumb'. A set of rules were tabulated and approved, with one of the main objects being *'To afford to its members facilities for intellectual, moral and religious improvement.'*

The new Committee certainly moved at a cracking pace. One day later its officials were in place, with John Thomson elected President, Alex Strathern Secretary, James Paul Treasurer and James Hay Collector with a salary of 15s per week.

In discussion of the current state of the Deaf Community in Glasgow, it was felt that *'More energetic measures should be taken to raise funds for the purpose of obtaining the services of a properly qualified religious teacher, and that their requirements should be made known to the public and its assistance solicited.'* With a view to doing so more effectively, they resolved to visit several of the leading clergymen to obtain their co-operation.

In November, a deputation argued the case for a Minister for the Deaf in Glasgow to the Directors of the Langside School. The Directors proposed that this 'Missionary' to be appointed *'Should employ part of his time each Sabbath evening at the Institution in giving the children Bible lessons, and it return for this, they would contribute annually a like sum to that contributed by the Deaf and Dumb themselves.'*

It was also proposed that William Crawford, Collector for the Langside Institution should also act as Collector for the Society and that the services of the unfortunate James Hay be dispensed with. This was approved, and it seems to have been a most effective appointment, for by the end of 1873, he had succeeded in raising the balance of Society funds to £300.

All was not sweetness and light within the Committee however. Clearly internal politics and power struggles were raising their ugly heads.

At a Meeting in May 1873, the Minutes indicate that *'A misunderstanding which had arisen in the minds of certain members of the Committee was explained. The said members however tendered their resignations, which were accepted.'* Alex Strathern also offered his resignation, but was *'Prevailed upon by the general wish to withdraw it again.'* Obviously a major schism had occurred amongst the Committee, causing John Heggie and John and James Elliott to resign.

Almost as a footnote (after the vacancies had been filled) it was proposed by Mr Strathern, clearly not taken aback at his near resignation, that Mr James Howard (who was Assistant Teacher at the Edinburgh Institution) *'Was a fit and proper person to be appointed Missionary of the Deaf and Dumb of Glasgow.'*

This was accepted unanimously.

The appointment of Howard seems very likely to have been the cause of the conflict. There is no mention previously of his application, and it is probable that the resigning Directors either objected to his appointment or the haste with which it was proposed. No doubt they felt 'bounced' into making the appointment. It would seem that Alex Strathern (and his faction) were the prime movers in seeking Mr Howard.

Minutes from a Meeting in September make it clear that the controversy still raged on. It was felt that *'It would be best to let the Directors send for Mr Howard so that the Deaf and Dumb Committee might be free from all suspicion of arbitrary selection in case of future complaints.'* No doubt they had foreknowledge of trouble ahead.

Then is revealed one of the objections (or the main objection) to Howard's appointment. *'Mr McCaig was not sure as to the advisability of having an Episcopalian to conduct services for a Presbyterian Congregation. Mr Strathern said that Mr Howard would conduct the service precisely as at present conducted. He did not see any objection to a properly qualified Missionary, whatever Denomination he might belong to.'*

The controversy was not ended: at the next Meeting of members, a good old fashioned 'Rammy' occurred, in which some protested that the membership had not been consulted in regard to the appointment. One member, Mr Kinnock, had gone to the extent of writing to the Secretary of Langside School, stating that the Deaf and Dumb did not approve of Mr Howard. There may be a slight indication here that there was a genuine split between some deaf members and the mainly hearing Directors. However after William Agnew in the Chair had chided Mr Kinnock as being *'A man of strife!'*, Mr Strathern affirmed that the appointment was sanctioned by members and asked for a show of hands in favour. He received *'A simultaneous raising of hands in favour.'*

Whether the Meeting was 'rigged' or whether this was, indeed, the general wish, or whether the ordinary members were simply tired of conflict, is hard to say. At last however, the Society had a Missionary, and it was about this time (November 1873) that the Society started terming itself 'The Glasgow Mission to the Deaf and Dumb'.

CHAPTER 2

TEMPERANCE, THRIFT AND TOIL

James Howard took up his post as Missionary on 1ˢᵗ January 1874. He set to work energetically, submitting Quarterly Reports on his progress to the Directors of the Society. Some excepts from these give interesting snapshots of the condition of the Deaf in Glasgow at that time:-

'During the Quarter I have visited upwards of 80 of the Deaf and Dumb at their own homes - some of them frequently as necessity required. Some of these I find very poor indeed and rarely receiving visits from Clergymen or Missionaries and attending no place of worship. I obtained promises from many of these to attend the services for the Deaf and Dumb. But only in few cases have they fulfilled their promises.

On the other hand, I find a great many living in respectable houses and respectable in themselves, and also in communion with the various churches of the city, but these I find with few exception as those who live with speaking relatives, or who stay with special friends. I find many of those who are married - the husband and wife both being deaf and dumb, are much lower in the social scale than those who live with speaking relatives or friends .... I find in certain quarters much drunkenness prevailing. This I have endeavoured to combat by persuasion to sign a pledge of Total Abstinence, and I have obtained the signatures of 6 persons much given to drink. I am not yet able to speak of the results of this with the exception of one case which is in every way satisfactory. The desire for company which is very great in the Deaf and Dumb is a source of many being led away, being attracted to houses where many congregate and where drinking is prevalent. This I think might be obviated to a great extent could we obtain a room to the used as a Reading Room, and where games of draughts, chess etc could be introduced. They would thus be drawn together where there could be little or no evil influences, and from this it would be an easy matter to lead them to the services.' (April 20ᵗʰ 1874).

However as Howard was to find, the road to Salvation was often a bumpy one, or in this case there was many a slip 'Twixt pub and pledge:-

'In my last report I mentioned that I had endeavoured to combat the habits of drunkenness which prevail amongst many of the Deaf and Dumb, by persuasion to sign a pledge of Total Abstinence. I regret to find that this has so far proved a failure. Out of 6 who took the pledge, 4 kept it for 3 days and the other 2 for 3 months.' (August 3rd 1874).

Howard, however did achieve a substantial increase in attendance at services. But, in spite of this, and all the strife generated by his appointment, Howard resigned from his post in July 1874. He had been successful in obtaining the post of Head Teacher at the Yorkshire Institution for the Deaf and Dumb in Doncaster. It may be that he found his task in Glasgow too daunting, but it is probably more likely that he was first and foremost an Educationalist.

In spite of his early resignation, he in many ways set much of future direction of the Society.

The Committee wasted no time in appointing a Successor. Frederick Woodbridge, Missionary to the Deaf and Dumb at Oldham was 'Headhunted', and invited to conduct a service. His performance was met with general approval. William Agnew remarked that he was *'Much struck by Woodbridge's power of expression in the sign language.'*

Learning from recent experience, the appointment was first ratified at a General Meeting of members. Any thought of delay amongst the Directors was removed by the intelligence that Woodbridge had the offer of another post. Accordingly, the appointment was confirmed in October 1874.

On Woodbridge's appointment, the Committee set about formalising and expanding the work of the Society. A Constitution was drawn up, and galvanised by Woodbridge, major plans to extend the work of the Society were laid.

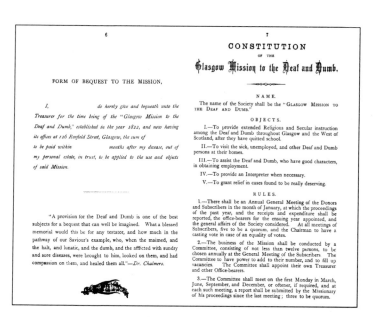

1ˢᵗ Society Constitution

A Debating Class had already been established, meeting in Whyte's Temperance Hotel during the winter months. According to Woodbridge, writing in 1875:- *'A Debating Class was held last year amongst the members with rather unsatisfactory results. Much disorder and ill-feeling arose from very insignificant causes, several trying to speak at once, and at last I was obliged to retire from it. Several of the members became so offended by this that they resolved to stay away from our Sabbath services and weekday meetings and have not been since. However I drew up a Code of Rules, and since that time the meetings have been very orderly and well conducted, and the members have shown much good will and equanimity under defeat, although occasionally the powerful arguments of an opponent appear to ruffle the temper considerably.'* The Debating Club was not the first of the Society's clubs. That honour belongs to the Football Club, which was founded by ex pupils of the Langside School for Deaf (and members of the Society) in 1871, making the club the oldest Deaf Football Club in the World.

The players of Queen's Park F.C. (founded in 1863: the oldest Senior Football Club in Scotland) used the playing fields at the Langside School for training. No doubt stimulated by their example, a group of ex-pupils of the School, prominent amongst whom was William Agnew, founded Glasgow Deaf and Dumb F.C. Originally, due to the lack of other clubs, they played and practised amongst themselves, wearing colours of a red and yellow hooped semmit and white trousers.

To address the main perceived problems of the Deaf:- *'Many of the Deaf and Dumb are very improvident in prosperity, and when adversity strikes are left without means of subsistence .... many are addicted to intemperance.'* It was urgently proposed to open a Penny Savings Bank, Library and Newsroom, and to establish a course of Lectures: the rationale of Woodbridge being:- *'Could we provide for them intelligent and rational amusement, I have no doubt that they would gradually be drawn away from the Public House and eventually led to become part of our Sabbath congregation.'*

The major stumbling block to these laudable objectives was the lack of premises, but by 1875 accommodation was secured by hiring a hall at 126 Renfield Street for a rent of £33 per Annum.

Discussions were entered into with the view to extending the work of the Society to Paisley and it was decided that the Missionary would establish a service in U.P. Church in Canal Street.

Woodbridge also initiated a programme of Addresses to the children at the Langside Institution on Sunday evenings.

Bemoaning previous problems experience by the Deaf with regard to Communion, Woodbridge arranged the first Communion Service wholly for the Deaf at the Anderston Church. He revealed his ultimate goal in his summary at the end of the 1874 Report:- *'I trust the time is not far distant when this Society will take its proper position among the Philanthropic Societies of the day, and when Glasgow, alive to the work that is required of her, and recognising this urgent want of these afflicted people, will become the second city in Great Britain which can boast of possessing a Church for the Deaf and Dumb.'*

The 1874 Report includes examples of how the lot of some of the Deaf in Glasgow now benefited from the work of the Society:-

---

13

A FEW OF THE CASES BENEFITED BY THE SOCIETY

1. A very dissipated young man, the cause of great grief to his widowed mother, was induced to take the pledge of total abstinence, and now great hopes are entertained of his becoming quite exemplary in his habits.

2. This man (wife also deaf & dumb) was found in a most destitute condition; two daughters grown up, and all doing nothing. Parish relief was obtained for them, and they were exhorted to bestir themselves. One of the daughters soon found work, and a situation was shortly afterwards found for the father.

3. This young man, a joiner, the principal support of his mother, who is a widow, broke his leg at a football match, and was thus thrown out of employment for a long time The sum of £3 was subscribed amongst the members for him.

4. A very poor girl not brought up to any trade, but assisted her mother in sewing wheat bags,-a hard and poorly paid employment. When visited she was in a wretched condition; she had no boots, and was only just shielded from the cold. After several days had been spent in seeking more suitable employment for her, Mr. Alexander, of Calton, very kindly undertook to provide her with what tools she required, and to teach her the trade of stay-making with whom she is now doing well.

5. Two brothers, both deaf and dumb, and both quite young, left their father's roof, thinking they would be much better off, as they could then spend all their wages upon themselves. On returning for their clothes, and telling their father of their determination never to live at home again, he became very angry, and kicked them rather severely. They left, and went into lodgings. After much trouble they were prevailed upon to return home; and the father promised to treat them better in future.

6. A plate of iron fell upon this young man's right foot about eight months ago. He was sent to the Sea-side Home for a time, and apparently recovered; the only effect left being a little lameness. His situation was filled up, and he was out of work for a long time. At last another situation was got for him; but he could not take it, as his knee began to swell, and he was obliged to keep his bed. As it got worse, Dr Orr's advice was obtained, and he recommended his removal to the Royal Infirmary. Messrs. Lees & Anderson kindly gave a subscriber's note, and he was sent there on Christmas Day.

A few of the cases benefitted - 1874

From these cases one starts to gain a vivid impression of what life was like for some of the Deaf in Victorian Glasgow.

It was a tribute to the work of the Missionary and the Directors that in the 1875 Report Woodbridge was able to state:- *'Most of the hopes shadowed forth, and promises made in our last Report, have been realised and fulfilled to the letter, and the mission has now not only a habitation and a name, but a Penny Bank has been established, a Reading Room opened, a Library is in the course*

13

of formation, weekly Prayer Meetings are held, and last but not least - the first session of a highly instructive and interesting course of Lectures has just come to a close.'

The Reading and News Room at the new premises was supplied with 2 daily papers;-'The Mail' and 'Evening Citizen'; 2 weekly papers:- 'The Graphic' and 'Chatterbox'; and 4 monthly:- 'Good Words', 'Chambers Journal', 'British Workman' and 'Band of Hope'. In addition, Chess, Draughts, Dominoes and a Bagatelle Table were provided. The Library had an initial stock of 200 books and was expanding.

The Penny Savings Bank paid interest of 5% on all sums deposited for a year, with deposits only allowed to be withdrawn after 3 months: all designed *'To counteract the habits of Improvidence and to lead them in time to habits of Frugality.'* Twenty three depositors were attracted initially, with almost £10 being deposited. As a further incentive to saving, the following rhyme was displayed:-

> *'Not for to hide it in a hedge,*
> *not for a train attendant,*
> *but for the glorious privilege*
> *of being Independent.'*

The first Winter programme of lectures also got off to a successful start - including such diverse topics as:- 'Scenes from Scottish History', 'Notes of a Tour in India (Illustration by dissolving views)', 'Water with Experiments', 'Varieties of the Human Race' and 'Alcoholic Brain Poison'. Most of the learned guest speakers delivered the lectures orally, with signing provided by an interpreter. It was therefore possible for hearing friends of the Deaf to attend: an entirely new venture.

It can therefore be seen that many of the social and moral objectives of the Society were beginning to be met; though the occasional unanticipated problem did arise:-

'Some of the members complained that they could not see my hands on account of the twinkling of the gas, and when they stood up for prayer, others taller than themselves occupied the places in front. I at once got 2 white globes fixed on the burners in front of my desk and I have had a small platform made about 9 inches high on which I stand when addressing them and much satisfaction has resulted from this arrangement.' (September 1876).

The number of services for the Deaf had also increased, with 4 special Communion services and a series of weekly prayer meetings in the new Hall.

The Society, through the catalyst of the Missionary, had clearly now been imbued in the Zeitgeist of the Age of Reform, and set about with increasing gusto in tackling the problem of Unemployment amongst the Deaf. Woodbridge, writing in the 1876 Report writes frankly about the difficulties he experienced in trying to secure jobs for Deaf members:-

'Owing to the long and unusual Depression in Trade, I had numerous applications for work, and much time was spent in going from place to place with these applicants in the hope of obtaining Employment for them. Several days and sometimes weeks were spent in fruitless search. Having succeeded with more than 20 of them at a most trying time, embracing the following trades:- Painters, Caulkers, Joiners, Gilder, Confectioner, French Polisher, Labourers, Cap Winder, Tailor, Shoemaker, Cabinetmaker, Hammerman, Boxmaker etc. I take this opportunity to render sincere acknowledgements to Messrs Napier and Son, Messrs Elder, Messrs Barclay Curle and Co, Messrs Wylie and Lochead, Messrs Scott and other firms who have kindly given employment to the Deaf and Dumb on my application.

No prejudice against the Employment of the Deaf and Dumb workmen exists with these firms; but with some masters I find considerable difficulty in overcoming this feeling. Even when there has been a good opening for a man, as soon as they become aware that the applicant is Deaf and Dumb, they respectfully but firmly decline to engage him. I trust that a clearer knowledge of the capacities of Deaf and Dumb workmen will in time become more widely spread amongst employers of labour, as I feel assured were the facts really known it would have a great tendency to remove this ill-founded prejudice, and often place the Deaf and Dumb on an equality with others.'

In other ways too the Society was expanding its range of activities. It held its first Annual Excursion of members on 26th August 1876. The destination was Stirling and around 60 members:- *'Availed themselves of the opportunity to visit that Ancient Burgh, which is as remarkable for its natural beauty as it is rich in historical associations. Field sports occupied most of the morning, and the whole of the afternoon was taken up in visiting the Castle, Abbey Craig, and other objects of interest in the area.'*

Another long lived tradition of the Society was also established that year:- the New Year Supper for the Poor, which was held in the Mission Hall on 3rd January. As to what constituted the contemporary criteria of Poverty is not mentioned; but *'Between 25 and 30 who had had free tickets sent to them, partook of the treat, consisting of plum puddings etc - the funds for this being subscribed amongst the members (£43/18/2d had been raised for the poor fund.) The doors were thrown open at 7 o'clock to all comers, and the room became quite crowded. All were then regaled with as much fruit, sweets etc as they chose to take. Mr White of Sauchiehall Street lent a large Stereoscope with about a hundred glass slides, and an electric machine which added considerably to the pleasures of the evening.'*

There was no doubt that the Annual Soiree, first held in 1856, was regarded as the most important event of the year; a chance to acknowledge the achievements and advances made by the Society, to entertain and inform and most importantly to exhort the members to even higher things.

The 1876 Meeting was congratulated on the prosperous condition of the Society, thence:- *'Several recitations, charades, and a well arranged piece were then capitally performed by the members.'*

Then to the main rally call of the evening, and one close to Woodbridge's heart:- an Appeal for funds for a Church. Woodbridge called attention to the Societies of London and Manchester: London's Church having already been completed and the latter having raised £5,000 by 'An Immense Bazaar', and the Church now almost erected.

'Now', he concludes, *'is there any reason why Glasgow should remain behind? None! Let her then follow the example of the 2 pioneers - London and Manchester: set her shoulders to the wheel, and no doubt in a few years we should see a place of worship erected for our Deaf and Dumb which would be a credit to the City.'*

Good rousing stuff this: appealing not just to the religious zeal, but also to the civic pride of the members and dignitaries present. One can imagine the resounding ovation to these noble exhortations. It seems to have been effective too, as that year £200 - a very tidy sum indeed, was transferred to the Building Fund.

This quest for a Church for the Deaf was the Holy Grail of the day, but every-day provision for the spiritual needs of the members was expanded to include a Bible Class for the Young - started in February 1876 by John Heggie and boasting an initial attendance of 13.

The Missionary also ministered to sick and dying members as Woodbridge testifies:-

'I was informed on the Sabbath that he was sinking fast, so I got a gentleman to take my place, and spent the evening with him. He had not attended our services regularly for some time previous, nor been seriously inclined, yet God was gracious to him at the Eleventh Hour, and as I left him his last words were - 'I am going to my last home to be with Christ for ever' .... *'On the 3ʳᵈ and 13ᵗʰ of the same month, 2 bright little girls, Margaret and Catherine, daughters of Mr Lindsay of Govan, were cut down by Scarlet Fever - Lambs of Christ's Flock called early home to the Fold.'*

Having encouraged Thrift and Toil, Temperance, the next great Pillar of Victorian Society was aspired to. An incident from 1875 gives a small insight into the extent of the problem:-

'A girl was lately imprisoned for drunkenness. She was visited before her term expired, and it was ascertained that she had run away from home (Campbelltown) *7 or 8 months ago, and came to Glasgow, where she had led a most dissolute life ever since* (no doubt she had been involved in Prostitution also). *It was proposed to the Chaplain of the Prison that she should be taken back to her parents, with the hope that it would be a turning point in her life. This being agreed to, the Missionary took her home, and prevailed upon her*

16

mother to take her back, although very reluctant to do so. A letter has since been received from her, which stated that she was helping her mother in domestic duties, and had not tasted intoxicating drinks since she was taken home.'

The key to this small success and others like it was, it was seen, Temperance.

Glasgow of the day was in some respects a prosperous city; seen by some as the Second City of the Empire. The distribution of wealth, however, meant that the vast bulk of the populace lived a mean and miserable existence. This was the Glasgow of Cholera and Tuberculosis epidemics, prostitution,public drunkenness and filthy, overcrowded conditions (though by now some improvements had been made in Public Health due to the new Public Water Supply being piped from Loch Katrine). The 'Demon Drink' was regarded as a scourge akin to the way we regard Heroin Addition in our Society.

A contemporary statistic is revealing:- on an average Saturday night in Glasgow it was estimated that around 1,500 people were carried insensible from the streets on police hand carts. Such was the effect of an evening in the Shebeens and Public Houses.

This situation was not unique to Glasgow. Most Victorian towns and cities of the day had districts where this was the norm. A description of the Canongate in Edinburgh in 1880, written by Alexander Smith in the classic travelogue 'A Summer in Skye' is most revealing:-

'But the Canongate has fallen from its High Estate. Quite another race of people are its present inhabitants. The vices to be seen are not genteel. Whisky has supplanted claret. Nobility has fled, and squalour has taken possession. Wild, half naked children swarm around every doorstep. Ruffians lounge about the mouths of the Wynds. Female faces, worthy of 'The Inferno', look down from broken windows. Riots are frequent; and drunken mothers reel past scolding white atomies of children that nestle wailing in their bosoms - little wretches to whom Death were the greatest benefactor .... The Fever Van comes frequently here to convey some poor sufferer to the Hospital. Hither comes the Detective on the scent of a Burglar. And when evening falls, and the lamps are lit, there is a sudden hubbub and crowd of people, and presently from its midst emerge a couple of policemen and a barrow with a poor, half-clad, tipsy woman from the Sister Island crouching upon it, her hair hanging loose about her face, her hands quivering with impotent rage, and her tongue wild with curses. Attended with small boys, who bait her with taunts and nicknames, and who appreciate the comic element which so strangely underlies the horrible sight, she is conveyed to the Police Cell, and will be brought before the Magistrate tomorrow - for the twentieth time perhaps - as a 'Drunk and Disorderly and dealt with accordingly'. (p18)

To combat this evil, the Temperance Society, one of the most long-lived Institutions within the Society, was launched in 1878; attracting initially only 5 members. But by 1879, 27 members had 'Signed the Pledge'. The Missionary writes:- *'All total Abstainers, doing their utmost to cope with the gigantic evil of Intemperance which presents such a terrible opposition to all efforts for Good.'*

FOR MEMBERS.	The Glasgow Deaf and Dumb Temperance Association.
	Established 1878.
✗ ✗ ✗	ROYAL INSTITUTE, 158 W. Regent St.
	Hon. Directors.
	Mr. WILLIAM JAMES WOOD.
	Rev. JOHN HENDERSON.
Attend all Meetings.	Mr. DONALD DEWAR.
	Mr. GEORGE NICHOLSON.
Endeavour to induce others to join.	**Lady Directors.**
	Mrs. SCOTT MATHESON.
Never be afraid to say " No."	Mrs. W. WRIGHT.
" Be not among Wine-Bibbers."	**Hon. President.**
	Mr. WILLIAM WRIGHT.
There is danger in the glass.	**President**—Mr. J. SINCLAIR
	Vice-President— Mr. T. HUNTER
	Hon. Secretary—Mr. W. H. DUFF.
	Hon. Treasurer—Mr. J. CARRUTHERS.
	Committee.
	Messrs. T. Sutherland, Geo. Geddes,
	J. Richardson, A. B. Middleton, and
Keep Your Pledge!	Alex. Maclean.
	Ladies' Committee.
	Mrs. J. Carruthers, Mrs. W. H. Duff,
	Misses Jeanie Scott, Kate Wilson,
	and Tina Dougal.

Temperance Society Membership card

1878 was a year of great import for the Society, in that a new Missionary, John Henderson, was appointed. Frederick Woodbridge, having been extremely instrumental in expanding the Society's Institutions, responding perhaps to a call of the Wild, or a need for a fresh challenge or maybe an increased salary, left the Society in August 1878 to take up the post as Head of the Institution for the Deaf in Halifax, Nova Scotia.

Within a short time, John Henderson, formerly a teacher at Donaldson's Hospital in Edinburgh, was appointed as Missionary.

Welcoming Henderson, and introducing him as Missionary, Dr. Aikman, perhaps rattled by the unexpected departure of Woodbridge, injected a note of caution in his Address, saying that no doubt they had made a happy choice and that he hoped they would never have cause to repent of it. His caution proved to be entirely misplaced.

The same year also saw great challenges to the Society; not just because of the upheaval caused by the departure of the Missionary, but also Economic

18

Depression or 'Great slackness of Trade' and the consequent high Unemployment amongst the Deaf. Much more money had to be spent on relief, and an approach to the City Benevolent Society resulted in the contribution of 5 shillings worth of Bread Tickets weekly.

Great efforts were made in 1879 to improve matters for the Unemployed and Destitute Deaf. Some members, notably a Mrs Hay, who often accompanied Henderson on his visits to the Poor, supplied clothing, boots and blankets, as well as money. A great deal more was raised for the poor fund, leaving a surplus of £6 at the end of the year. Clearly there were great efforts in general fundraising and raising the public profile of the Society in that year.

Perhaps, through the personality of the new Missionary, or through the changing economic conditions, there seems to have been a change of focus in the main aims of the Society, since in the conclusion of the 1879 Report there is no exhortation towards a prime objective of a Church for the Deaf.

It is abundantly clear that John Henderson's arrival, as in Woodbridge's first years, saw a galvanising influence on many aspects of the Society. As has been mentioned, fundraising seems to have been particularly fruitful, gaining the Society by 1880 a healthy surplus and its first ever legacy:- one of £500 from Matthew Muir.

The Society was expanding also. In this year a Branch was establish in Paisley, with the Glasgow Society supplying a regular Sunday Service. The Temperance Society had considerably raised its membership and its profile, boasting an increase to 35 members and with an ex Lord Provost as Patron. As a means of recruiting members it had held its first ever Annual Excursion to 'The beautiful and romantic Campsie Glen'.

The Football Club had already raised funds of £4.0s.5d for the Church Building Scheme. In June 1880 John Henderson wrote:- *'The members of the Football Club connected with the Mission have resolved to utilise their services in the way of raising money in aid of the Building Fund by playing matches with other teams.'*

The Annual Soiree gives some insight into the Great Debate of the day (and probably ever since) as to whether the purely Oralist system was superior to the Manual system of Signing. It is clear that differences of opinion existed within the Society's own Committee and Directors. The Annual Soiree seems to have been the vehicle for propounding viewpoints on this.

At the 1876 Soiree the Rev Dr. Aikman praised the Oral system of Teaching. But in the 1877 Report, Woodbridge the Missionary draws attention to the importance of the Finger and Sign Language in worship:- *'The Finger and Sign Language which forms this special provision is fortunately as effective as the voice. With it, Preaching, Prayer and Praise are available; without it, quite impossible.'*

At the 1880 Soiree, the Chairman Henry Watson (with Aikman also on the platform party) *'Then spoke of the Lip System of Education, in regard to which he said that even its warmest supporters allowed that it never could become universal as a means of enabling the Deaf and Dumb to understand an ordinary Church Service.'* One can perhaps imagine the Rev Dr. Aikman looking daggers behind his back.

Criticism within the Society of the Oral System at that time, can be seen then as limited to the Religious sphere.

But it should be noted that in 1876 the question of introducing the Oral System was considered at the Langside School:-

'In the Autumn, 2 of the Directors, along with Headmaster, visited 9 schools in England in which that method of teaching had been tried. The result of their visit was that in the following year a beginning was made in the System, classes being formed with 50 pupils in all.

It is well known that Educationists are divided into those who advocate an exclusively Oral System, those, (probably a very small number) who reject that System altogether, and those who think that a course of Education in which the Manual and the Oral system are both employed according to circumstances, yields the best results, looking to the interests of the children as a whole and the time available for their instruction.

The Directors of the Institution came to the conclusion that the Oral Method should be tried, so far as was practicable, with all the children, recognising the Physical benefit to be derived from the muscular movements involved, even in the case of those who showed little aptitude, but that to spend time on those who showed no aptitude at all, which might be better devoted to teaching them in the old way, was only to waste it. Accordingly it was decided to continue the Education of the children on the Dual Basis, and this policy has been continued ever since.' (Penney p15-17)

It was to the credit of the Langside School that at least it was not wholly carried away on the tide of Oralism beginning to sweep the world, culminating in the infamous 'Congress of Milan' in 1880, at which a body of influential, though by no means representative Educators of the Deaf passed 2 crucial resolutions:-

'1 The Congress, considering the incontestable superiority of speech over signs, for restoring Deaf Mutes to social life and for giving them greater facility in language, declares that the method of articulation should have preference over that of signs in the instruction and education of the Deaf and Dumb.

2 Considering that the simultaneous use of signs and speech has the disadvantage of injuring speech, lipreading and precision of ideas, the Congress declares that the pure Oral Method ought to be preferred.'

After this, the Manual Method was virtually proscribed in Schools for the Deaf throughout the World - In some schools which adopted Pure Oralism,

Deaf children who attempted to sign were forced to sit on their hands or, if they persisted, had their hands tied behind their backs. (Dimmock p32).

At the 1880 Soiree, Watson was also critical of new technological advances to assist the Deaf:-

'In noticing the newly invented Audiphone, he said that, although it had received a good deal of Yankee puffing, as far as he could learn it was practically useless for the great majority of Deaf persons.'

Injecting a lighter note into proceedings and anticipating the long tradition of Drama in the Society, was a Burlesque performed by several amongst the Audience: *'So replete with fun that it kept the Audience in the height of glee during the whole of the Performance.'*

Drama was now beginning to be established as an essential part of the Society's activities with one of the highlights of the year being the Performance at the Annual Soiree. In 1881 an Eastern Burlesque entitled 'Blue Beard, Bearded and Defeated, or the Triumph of Love' gained the praise:- *'They deserve credit for having in the particular raised themselves to a level with their Hearing Brethren.'* High praise indeed. Credit was also due to William Rendall, 'Who for some time has been giving them lessons in this harmless entertainment.'

In 1881 there was evident dissatisfaction with the premises of the Society - now too small for its increasing areas of activity. Mr G. Kerr referred to *'The growing sympathy shown by the Public for the Deaf and Dumb'*, but continues that he *'Hoped this sympathy would soon take a practical shape in providing a better hall than the present one.'*

In terms of finances that year, all was most certainly not sweetness and light. As John Henderson states tersely in his Report:- *'The Mission has suffered considerable loss through the defalcations of the late Collector Mr William Crawford.'* The Annual Balance Sheet reveals a loss of £88.10.0d, offset by the recovery of £22.8.5d from Crawford's Estate. Clearly the now deceased Collector had been 'Cooking the Books' for some time. However due to legacies and the efforts of Archiebald Goold, the new collector, by 1882 a surplus of £137 was in hand.

The Society at this period had developed into a remarkably self confident Organisation; illustrated by the Report on the Annual Excursion of 1882:- *'The members had their Annual Excursion on Saturday 9th September, Tillietudlem Castle being the place of resort. About 70 left Glasgow, and this number was largely augmented by friends who joined at the various stations en route. On arrived at the grounds various games were engaged in. Through the liberality of Lord Provost Ure, Sir William Collins, James White Esq, Walter McFarlane Esq, Mrs Pearce, Miss Lyle and the Misses Forgie, handsome prizes were given. Before leaving, a lively scene took place - the Smokers and the Non-*

Sports at the Annual Excursion were very much a Society tradition. 3-Legged Race; early 1900's

Smokers engaging in a Tug-o-War when the Advocates of the Weed were forced to acknowledge themselves beaten. It was a very enjoyable day.'
By 1883 the frustrations of the previous few years concerning the inadequacy of the Society's premises were abated by the rental of new Hall, dubbed 'Hope Hall', at 65a Renfrew Street, which was opened by the Rev Aikman on 3rd June 1883, and described as:- *'Our new and commodious premises, comprising a Hall, Recreation Room, Committee Room and an Office, have given every satisfaction.'*
It is clear that Hope Hall did not represent the limit of the Society's aspirations, as a sum of £887-15-8d remained in the Building Fund: as to whether it was primarily targeted towards a Church or larger new premises is not clear.
There is no doubt that the Society had a strong commitment to expansion into other areas. Funds had been raised for the appointment of an Assistant Missionary, Joseph Foster, whose remit was principally to minister to the surrounding districts:- *'It is hoped that under his care the work of the Mission will be largely extended, and that those of the Deaf and Dumb whom distance has debarred from the privilege of Public worship will be specially benefited.'*
Paisley Mission was by now up and running, having procured a hall of their own and providing games and reading materials for its members.
A new initiative within the Society was the formation of an Ambulance Class under the St Andrew's Ambulance Association. This was the first such class ever instituted by the Deaf. The catalyst for its formation seems to have

22

been a Lecture and Demonstration given by a Dr. Nairne to the Society. Initially the class attracted 16 young Deaf men, who undertook to study for their Ambulance Certificates.

As it proved, the Class was to be extremely successful. On Examination in May 1885, all students (now risen to a total of 25) passed with flying colours, with the Examiner commenting that their knowledge of Anatomy and their handling of a supposed injured person were admirable and that he had never examined a Class with greater pleasure.

The pace of expansion continued, partly due to the appointment of the Assistant Missionary. A Branch of the Society in Hamilton was formed in May 1885, having been granted free use of the Mining Institute Hall.

The Assistant Missionary, Joseph Foster, conducted alternative Services in Hamilton and Paisley. Moves were afoot to form a branch at Greenock and by 1890 a Branch had been established in Govan. A Branch was also formed in Dumfries, though Services had not yet been established, but the granting of free First Class Railway Passes by the Directors of the Glasgow and S.W. Railway enabled both the Missionary and Assistant Missionary to visit regularly, making educational provision for some Deaf children and finding work for the Unemployed Deaf. Helping the Unemployed was in many ways the greatest service the Society could perform on the ground for the Deaf. The Economy remained depressed. The Society distributed small sums for temporary relief; clothing, bread tickets, courtesy of the City Benevolent Society, and now soup tickets, courtesy of the Charity Organisation Society. The Missionary obtained employment for 33 individuals, gained Tax remittance for those unable to pay, and located a number of Deaf children not benefiting from Education.

The Temperance Society flourished, now boasting a membership of 69 (though some had broken the Pledge), enjoying lectures on subjects such as 'Great Men', 'Temperance Reformers', 'How I became an Abstainer', and obviously for strong constitutions only:- 'A Bar Room and what was seen there'.

Lectures for the Society in general were much more educational:- 'Curiosities of Zulu Life (illustrated by weapons of war, ornaments etc), 'Ancient Rome and its People', 'The Land we live in and other Views (Illustrated by Magic Lantern)', 'Debate:- Does Lord Salisbury deserve the confidence of his people?'.

In view of these activities, it is clear that the Society was well on the way to achieving its objective of being *One of the most necessary and useful Societies in the country*', as John Henderson stated in commending the Society for public support.

Clearly there was some internal conflict over Social Activities however, as the following excerpt from the Minutes of 1885 reveals:- *'Dr. Macleod moved that it is incompetent under the Constitution for the Directors to sanction Dancing in their Mission Hall. It was further agreed that the Annual Entertainment must henceforth be held in the name of private individuals, and altogether apart from the Mission or Directors.'*

In spite of this, Summer Outings seem to have been enjoyed much as normal, as John Henderson reports:- *'On 14th June the members had an Excursion to Cadder per a Steam Barge kindly lent by the Carron Company. On 28th to Carmyle, and on 30th August, a Trip to Millport.'*

The Society, though, had obviously been losing out on contributions due to continued confusion between it and the Langside School for Deaf children, as there appears for the first time the following Addenda to the 1885 Report:-

---

𝔊lasgow 𝔐ission to the 𝔇eaf and 𝔇umb,

65 RENFREW STREET.

This Society was Instituted in the year 1822, for the benefit of the **ADULT** Deaf and Dumb. It is distinct from the Institution at **Cathcart**, which is purely **Educational.**

By 1887, the Society seems to have decided that the main thrust of its fundraising was to provide *'A Meeting Place of their own, worthy of the Second City of the Empire.'* It was decided that a feasibility study of potential designs should be undertaken. Peat and Duncan the architects were appointed, and by 1888 they had prepared plans costed at £3,500. Since the building fund stood at £1,200, major fundraising initiatives were required.

Forms for special donations were drawn up. The problem of public confusion over the work of the Society and that of the Langside School was addressed by red lettering the word 'Adult' in fund raising material.

The Committee, however, were obviously still so perplexed by potential confusion, that they had, by 1890, altered the name of the Society in the Constitution to 'Glasgow Mission to the Adult Deaf and Dumb'.

'It was agreed to add the word 'Adult' to the title of the Mission, and also to get advertisement of the Institution (i.e. the Langside School) and the Mission side by side in the Post Office list of Charities.' - (10.3.90).

To secure new premises - the dream of 'The Proposed New Institute', no stone had been left unturned, and some very high profile supporters to the cause had been gained: none more so than the secural of the Patronage of Queen Victoria herself. By 1891, the Prince of Wales had consented to adopt the post of Honorary President, along with the Marquis of Lorne. One can perhaps imagine the influence exerted by the Queen on her erring eldest son 'Bertie' in this. The support of the Countess of Rosebery had also been secured.

She chaired '*A large and influential gathering in St. Andrew's Hall*', and during the year the large sum of £1,933 was raised; the Convenor of the Building Fund, William Agnew (also the probably founder of the Football Club) being particularly active.

The high profile of the Society extended beyond fundraising matters. In August 1889, the Rev Dr. Gallaudet, Son of the founder of the first American School for the Deaf, visited from New York and gave an Address to members.

In spite of the tribulations in trying to be recognised as the Champions of the Adult Deaf, the children of Deaf members were not neglected, and by 1891 one of the most enduring annual events in the Calendar of the Society; the Christmas Tree Entertainment, was established:-

'*A Christmas Tree Entertainment to all children of Deaf and Dumb parents took place on 25th December. Sir Chas Tennant provided an immense tree, and through the kindness of many friends, both Deaf and Dumb and Hearing, we were able to load it with good things. In addition to a substantial tea, each child was presented with several toys and useful articles, an orange, an apple, a parcel of sweets, a new penny and a Christmas card. A Magic Lantern, singing of hymns etc gave great enjoyment to the young folks. There were 75 children present, and a number of parents and friends. This meeting, suggested by Mr McCaig, is I believe, the first of its kind held in connections with any similar Mission, and we trust it will become an annual one.*'

Considering the poverty of the times, these gifts to the children seem extraordinarily generous and the whole event must have seemed truly magical to a poor child.

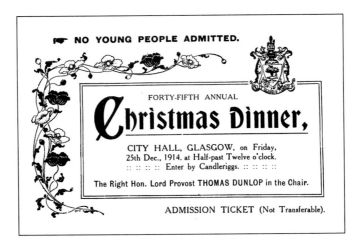

The Christmas Tree Entertainment complemented the already long established (since 1869) Christmas Dinner, from which children were excluded. The 1914 Dinner seems to have been a swell affair; though the ban on young people seems somewhat Scrooge like.

The Elderly, too, were not neglected. In 1891 a scheme was instituted to provide a fixed Yearly Allowance to Elderly and Infirm Deaf people; provided they were members of the Society or its Branches, had lived in the area for more than 7 years, and that they conducted themselves in a respectable and sober manner:- *'Any recipient found or known to be misbehaving repeatedly will forfeit his or her allowance.'* This scheme was later termed the Benevolent Society.

It was with a view to improving the welfare of the Poor (as well as increasing subscriptions), that led to the formation of the Ladies Auxiliary - one of the most important organisations within the Society. In early 1892, 31 ladies agreed on the main objectives of the new Society:- visiting the poor members, distributing clothing (the group responsible for this activity was named the Dorcas Society), and collecting subscriptions to the Society. The Duchess of Montrose agreed to become the President of the Auxiliary.

⤝⤞ ENTERTAINMENTS. ⤝⤞

Admission:—Berkeley Hall, 1s.; Cafe Chantant in Kent Hall, at 3-30 and 7 p.m., 6d.

Thursday's Programme.
Grand Hall, at 12 Noon.

Opening of Bazaar by Her Grace the Duchess of Montrose

Winkelmann's Grand Piano in Berkeley Hall, and Cottage Piano in Kent Hall, have been kindly lent by Messrs. J. MUIR WOOD & Co.

Grand Hall from 12-15 to 10 p.m. Also during Friday and Saturday.

Fortune-Telling in Gipsy Caravan, by Mrs. Cohen, the Zingara Queen.
Palmistry in Gipsy Caravan, by Miss Howard, the Romany Queen.
N.B.—As several large fortunes, amounting to millions, have been lying unclaimed at the Office of the Chancellor of the Exchequer for some time, it is expected that they will be judiciously allocated by the Gipsy Queens.
Character Delineated, and Pursuit of Life best adapted, pointed out through Phrenology, Astrology, and Sarcognomy, in Tent, by Captain J. Healy Fash, the "Sea King."
Portraits of Ye Oldyen Tymne, Cut while you wait, by Professor Carruthers.

The great fundraising event of 1891 was a Grand Bazaar, held in November over three days at St. Andrew's Halls. This was great feat of organisation and raised the substantial amount of £6,600 for the Building Fund. This, along with redoubled efforts from collectors and the ladies auxiliary enabled William Agnew, the Convenor of the Building Fund to write in 1893:-

'It is with great pleasure that we now inform our friends that the above Institute is just reaching the goal of erection .... on the splendid site at the corner of West Regent Street and West Campbell Street.'

Further details of the plan are revealed in the Directors' Minutes of 1892 and 1893:-

'The ground for the New Institute has been purchased for the sum of £4,500, and the purchase price paid over. The Estimates of cost of the New Institute sent in by the different Architects were submitted as follows:-

DESIGN	MR LEIPER'S ESTIMATE	ARCHITECT'S ESTIMATE
'POSTAGE STAMP'	£6,000 - £7,000	£4,000
'FITNESS'	£10,600	£4,000
'EPHPHATHA'	£11,000	£5,400
'LUCK'	£10,000 - £12,000	£6,000
'B'		£6,500

The high cost of some of these plans proved to a problem for some of the Directors and the Committee:-

'It was decided to ask from Mr Duncan, Architect, an amended plan, showing buildings not to cost over £4,000. Mr Duncan sent instead a plan, cost of which he estimated would be £4,500.'

This potential cost was more to everyone's liking:-

'Mr Kerr explained the steps taken by the Provisional Committee leading to the recommendation of the plan marked 'Ephphatha'. Unanimously agreed that Mr Duncan's Plan 'Ephphatha' be adopted.'

Detail: Ephphatha: Christ healing the Deaf man. Above the entrance to the Institute.

28

The plan was well named and particularly appropriate to the deaf. It is taken from a passage in St Mark's Gospel, in which Christ heals a Deaf man:- *'Jesus looked up to the sky and made a breathing sound. Jesus said to the man, 'Ephphatha'* (This is Aramaic for 'Be Opened'). *When Jesus did this, the man was able to hear. The man was able to use his tongue and spoke clearly.'* (Mark 7 v 34 - 35)

The Foundation Stone was laid in 1893. The dream of the Society that had seemed only half attainable and, in 1870 highly unlikely, was about to be realised.

Laying the Foundation Stone of the new Institute, 1893.
William Agnew, centre left : John Henderson, centre right.

CHAPTER 3
'A MEETING PLACE WORTHY OF THE SECOND CITY OF THE EMPIRE'

Woodcut, Royal Institute

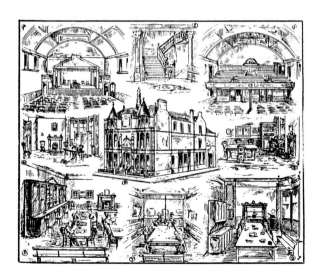

Plan of the interior.

The opening of the New Institute by Lord and Lady Blythswood in 1895 ushered in a new and even more self confident era in the Society's operations. The epithet 'Royal' had been bestowed by the Queen in 1897:- *'A letter was read from Lord Balfour, the Secretary of State for Scotland, intimating that H.M. The Queen has graciously acceded to our application to have the title 'Royal' incorporated in the name of our Institute.'*

Expansion in the number of Branches and Clubs was very much the order of the day. A Draughts Club was formed in 1897, a Girls Club was formed by the Ladies Auxiliary in 1900, and in 1904, a Y.M. and Y.W.C.A. was formed from the Bible Class. By 1905, the Y.M. and Y.W.C.A., meeting on Sunday evenings, had 91 on the roll. They enjoyed lectures on 'Notable Men and Women', raised funds for the Society, the New Benevolent Fund and held special Collections. (In 1905, they donated £1.5s to Benjamin Dickson, the Deaf Rothesay Street Artist. In fact, Benjamin had been a previous donor to the Society. In 1898, the Directors' Minutes record that:- *'The interesting donation of £1 came from a street artist Benjamin Dickson, who stays mostly in Rothesay. He is quite Deaf, very Blind and very Lame. Among his other pictures, he shows the Glasgow Institute and its Missionary, and the latest Union Liner 'The Briton'. Ben is a staunch Teetotaller and is continually trying to do good with his money.'*)

The Y.M. and Y.W.C.A had also established a special Library, held an Annual Social, a Picnic and several Summer Rambles. (A Rambling Club had been formed by the Bible Class in 1899).

Tableau Vivant:- a popular late Victorian/Edwardian entertainment in which evocative still scenes were recreated. 'Brigands Bold', 1896 Annual Soiree.

The Ladies Auxiliary Girls Club conducted special classes during the Winter, including a Physical Drill Class, a Sewing Class and an Ambulance Class. They concluded their Annual Programme with an 'At Home' and Tableau entertainment.

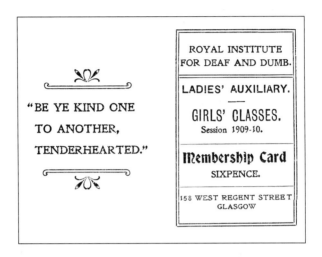

Girls Classes membership card.

Work at the Paisley Branch had been consolidated by following the example of Glasgow and the erection of a New Institute at 11 Queen Street, built at a cost of £1,600. The greatly expanded premises at the Royal Institute afforded scope for an increase in social activity. There was now a Reading Room, Library, Recreation Room, Billiard Room, Chess Room, Small Hall (now furnished with Gymnastic Apparatus) and Large Hall. An Annual Games Tournament was held comprising Billiards, Chess, Draughts, Bowling and Quoits. By 1906 the Chess and Draughts Club played for and won the Scottish Deaf and Dumb Chess and Draughts Trophy. The new Apparatus encouraged the formation of a Gymnasium Club which gave demonstrations to members in the Large Hall.

The splendid New Institute had also helped in attracting high profile guests to social occasions. The 1898 Annual Soiree was chaired by Lord Kelvin, the World renowned scientist:-

'The Annual Soiree of the Mission, Lord Kelvin presiding, was one of the most successful we have ever had. The play 'Cinderella' was thoroughly enjoyed by all. Lord and Lady Kelvin seemed highly interested and amused and his Lordship kindly sent a donation of £5 and expressed the pleasure he felt on his visit to the Institute.'

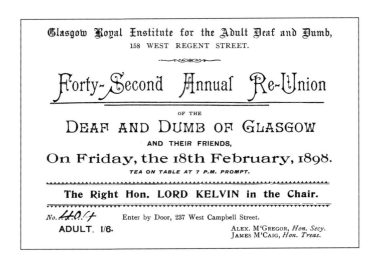

Annual Soiree (now termed Reunion) Invitation 1898.

The Football Club was also active socially and competitively. By 1901, the Club, then known as Blythswood Football Club or Blythswood Thistle were holding Annual Socials and Annual Picnics, visiting Arrochar in 1903. The Directors' Minutes of 1906 record that:- *'An unlikely event during the month was the Inter City Football Match between the Deaf and Dumb of Glasgow and Edinburgh for the Challenge Cup presented by Mr George Edwards for competition. The match took place at Motherwell, and the Glasgow Team won by 3 goals to 1.'*

By now the Ladies Auxiliary had established a large network of collecting areas and collectors. There were 41 Districts in 1905, reaching as far away as Bridge of Weir and Rothesay.

Funds were coming into the Society from special collections in various Hearing Sabbath Schools and Bible Classes. In a novel and imaginative move, the Society had the Manual Alphabet printed on cards and leaflets distributed amongst those attending these classes, thus potentially enabling better communication with the Deaf.

Busy though the Society was in expansion and fundraising, it was not unmindful of the current political situation. In 1900, the members had a lecture entitled:- 'Boers and Britons'; at which apparently, the bellicose warcry 'Boers - let 'em come!' was hurled by the speaker, somewhat carried away in militaristic fervour. Nonetheless it seems to have been effective, since the records state that the sum of £10 was contributed to the War Fund.

There was concern too, over the adverse effects of a recent Act of Parliament, resulting by 1906 in the following action:- *'Over 100 of the male members*

33

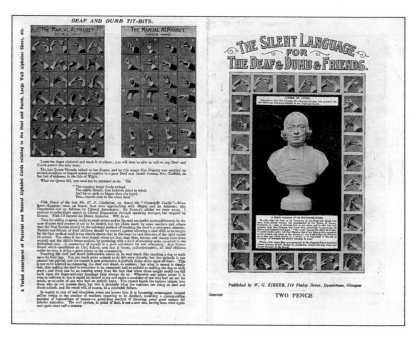

Manual Alphabet leaflets, c.1905 & 1920.

signed a petition in favour of having some alteration made in the 'Workmen's Compensation Act', so that the Deaf and Dumb would not be so handicapped.'

One of the most important developments of this era was that John Henderson was granted ordination by the United Presbyterian Synod in 1899. His job remained as challenging as ever though. He records in his report of 1901:-

'A fatal accident occurred to one of our members, John Hook, a heavy gate falling on him at the London and Glasgow Engineering Works, where he was employed. This is the only fatal accident to a Deaf Mute in this District during the last quarter of a Century, and it was rather remarkable that Mr Hook's wife had been married 3 times to Deaf Mutes and her other 2 husbands had also been killed by accidents.' Consoling this poor, unfortunate woman, who must have imagined that she was under some sort of curse, must have been one of the most demanding tasks of his career.

Other situations must have caused conflict between his humanity and the institutionalised Sectarianism of the day:- *'A number of Roman Catholic cases have applied for help, and it is rather difficult to know how to deal with them.'* (1.3.04). It is not recorded what help, if any, he proffered to these individuals.

His major task, though was striving to find work for the Unemployed Deaf. He writes in 1905:- *'Owing to the continued general Depression in Trade, an exceptional number of members have been idle, and a great amount of time has been spent daily in trying to find situations for them. The Telephone has proved of great use in this connection.'* After some initial suspicion, the Society had decided to embrace the new technology of the day - the equivalent of going 'On Line' today.

The Chairman of the Society, Major F.W. Allan, opens the 1907 Annual Report with these words:-

'The story of our Mission work from year to year does not present many new features to chronicle. The number of Deaf and Dumb in Glasgow and the West of Scotland remains about the same, and, as in former years, the object of the Mission has been to help them as far as possible in regard to their temporal and spiritual welfare. While the external evidence of the work has been satisfactory, it is hoped that the higher objects have also been attained to.'

In fact the pace of expansion had not slowed:- a new, but short-lived Branch opened at Motherwell, meeting at Hamilton Street Public School.

A snapshot of ongoing activities shows the range of the Society's efforts on behalf of the Deaf. Sabbath Services were held at the Royal Institute, the Branches and Langside. There was a Wednesday Prayer Meeting (which stated Allan 'Could be better attended'), and 2 Communions a year were celebrated. The Society received collections from 47 Churches, Bible Classes and Sunday Schools: the Deaf in some cases giving demonstrations using Manual Alphabet cards.

The Society distributed £90 in relief to poor members, provided over 300 items of clothing (the Dorcas Society of the Ladies Auxiliary distributed 60 new garments in addition), bread tickets were distributed, 167 bags of coal given out, the special benevolent fund provided pensions, and the Society obtained the free service of an Aurist, Oculist and a Dentist.

Home and Hospital visits had been made on 350 occasions by Elders, by the Ladies Auxiliary on 100 occasions, by the Y.M. and Y.W.C.A. 50 times and by the indefatigable Missionary, John Henderson, who visited 325 times and made 690 visits on behalf of the members. He also wrote 249 letters of introduction to Employers and found work for a total of 64 members.

The Royal Institute was open daily to all those who required advice or assistance. The Savings Bank flourished, the Temperance Association now had 189 members (the Womens Temperance Association, established in 1910 had by 1911 a membership of 92), and the Y.M./Y.W.C.A. had 41 members. The Girls Classes of the Ladies Auxiliary enjoyed instruction on sewing, art needlework, brasswork, cooking and sweet making.

With so many Branches in the surrounding area, it was decided it was appropriate in 1908 to term the Society 'Mission to the Adult Deaf and Dumb for Glasgow and the West of Scotland'; although the name 'Glasgow Mission to the Adult Deaf and Dumb' was retained in the Constitution.

Branches now existed at Hamilton, Govan, Motherwell, and now Bridgeton (established in 1909 at Green Street), and from 1912 at Coatbridge. Paisley was a Mission in its own right.

That year extensive repairs were necessary on the Institute buildings. Since the building was only 14 years old at that time, it makes one suspect that in the zeal and haste to complete the building, or indeed the desire to cut costs, perhaps a 'cowboy element' of the building trade may have been engaged. The need for repairs is glossed over somewhat:- *'Advantage has been taken of the opportunity this afforded to make several alterations and improvements, including increased heating facilities.'* All this is somewhat reminiscent of the Modern day Double-Speak, where defects or mistakes are termed as 'Improvement Opportunities'. It should be noted that the whole episode cost the Society the tidy sum of £900.

Financial strain due to the larger sums spent on relief were also placed on the Society with *'Strangers from all parts benefiting'* - though the Committee took care that:- *'Relief should only be given to cases really deserving, and have thus been enabled to help many to tide over their temporary distress without being forced to apply to the Parish.'*

The philosophy of the distribution of relief was firmly that:- *'The temporal welfare of the Deaf and Dumb is best promoted by inducing them to depend on their own labour, as far as possible, instead of trusting to claimable relief.'*

Long Live King George
Deaf members of the Society pledge their loyality to the new
Sovereign, King George V, c. 1911

The Enthronement of King George V saw the establishment of a new Branch Mission at Coatbridge, meeting at East Muiryhall Street Public School, Coatdyke.

The period of heightened political tension and rivalry with Germany and Central Powers, ultimately leading to World War 1, was not reflected in the Society's activities. Indeed in 1912 a lecture was given, seemingly in admiring terms, on 'Prince Bismarck, the Iron Chancellor'.

However, as might be expected, by 1914-15, the Society had evidently been caught up in the universal Pro-War, Anti-German mood: one lecture tellingly entitled:- 'The Huns.........', with other militaristic themes such as:-'The Story of the War', 'Napoleon Bonaparte', and 'King Arthur's Round Table', perhaps alluding to the nobility of the National Cause.

To aid the National Effort, the Society 'Not unmindful of the special need of the Country at the Present Crisis' raised £6.10.3d for the National Relief Fund, and the Women and Girls Guild sent parcels of knitted goods to 'The Minesweepers', and in 1916 additionally to interned British prisoners of War and Soldiers at Bellahouston Hospital.

The War too, saw part of the Royal Institute requisitioned:- *It was intimated that the Military Medical Board had hired the Small Hall and 2 subsidiary rooms at a rental of £75.'*

By 1916 there was the first hint of the realisation of the horrific implications of Modern Warfare, if not perhaps of the true extent of the carnage at the Front, in that the Society and no doubt other businesses accepted that the enemy had the capability to strike Civilians far beyond the Battlefields.

Fear of Zeppelin raids forced the Directors to take precautions:- *'It was agreed that the Institute and Tenement be insured against Air Raid damage.'* But the greatest damage to the Society during World War I was caused not by enemy bombs but by the death in December 1914 of the indefatigable William Agnew, who though wholly Deaf, had been the main guiding force behind the fundraising for the erection of the Royal Institute, and who had been a founding father of the Football Club.

By the Winter of 1916 possible Zeppelin raids had forced lighting restrictions, and this somewhat curtailed the Society's activities; forcing the cancellation of Winter Evening Services, the curtailment of the lecture programme and the cancellation of the meetings of the Women and Girls Guild (formerly the Girls Club). The girls though, doggedly continued at home their knitting for the Forces, with garments additionally sent to the Scottish Women's Hospital unit in Serbia, the Navy League and Stobhill Hospital.

The War also encouraged a more liberal approach in aid to the Poor:-

'Assistance from the Mission has been extended to .... Roman Catholics and to strangers in destitute circumstances.'

One of the long stated claims of the Society had been however:-

'The Mission is unsectarian in its character: its members belonging to several Christian Denominations. To be Deaf and Dumb entitles each applicant to its counsel and sympathy.'

Perhaps, as has been already suggested, this cherished ideal had not entirely been lived up to in the Pre-War period.

However by 1918, aid and ministry had been distributed to wounded troops invalided out of the Conflict, and a talk had been given to the Women and Girls guild on the Belgian Refugees in Glasgow.

It is clear, though, that there was hope for the Future and perhaps an end to that most cataclysmic conflict was glimpsed, as that year a Girls Hockey Club was formed, the Rambling Club reformed and a Literary and Debating Society was established, quickly achieving a membership of 80.

The period following the Armistice, which brought peace to the decimated ranks of Youth and to an exhausted World, heralded a turbulent period in the Society's History.

Initially there was trouble over a Legacy:- *'The Secretary reported regarding the Legacy of £200 bequeathed by the late Miss Mary Weild to 'The Deaf and Dumb Institution, Glasgow'. This Legacy is claimed on behalf of this Mission, and also on behalf of the Glasgow Society for the Education of the Deaf and Dumb. He explained that negotiations had taken place between the Societies and with a view to avoiding Litigation in regard to the matter, it had been arranged that the Legacy, when payable should be divided equally between them.'* Though this 'Judgement of Solomon' seems to have been effective on this occasion, persistent public confusion of the name of the Societies meant that there were many future similar problems over Legacies.

The Janitor at the Royal Institute had also caused somewhat of a scandal:- *'The Janitor had himself subsequently admitted that he had given drink to members of the Institute .... The Committee had no alternative but to accept his resignation.'* - (17.12.19)

In fact the position of Janitor seems to have been somewhat of a poisoned chalice since over the next ten years, the turnover of Janitors was no fewer than 6.

The main problem that the Society experienced in this period was a severe reduction in attendances at religious services. The problem was particularly acute at Branch level.

It is possible that this was a reflection of the general diminuation in Church attendance when the full realisation of the horrors of the War dawned on the populace at large. It may be also that, particularly in the Branches, unsuitability of premises may have been a factor.

However there is no doubt, as the following excerpts from the Minutes demonstrate, that the major cause was a crisis in the Missionaryship of the Society.

The first hint of crisis occurred in 1919:- *'The following resolution was moved by Mr W.G.E. Kirker:- 'That in view of the present incomplete system of visitation in Glasgow and throughout Lanarkshire, also of the great lack of variety in conducting the Sabbath Services, it is recommended that steps at once be taken to remedy these matters.'*

John Henderson by now had been Missionary of the Society since 1878, and was also acting as Secretary. The Society had expanded greatly since then, as had the City itself, and due to this, and his advancing age, it was seen in some quarters that his post, as it stood, was becoming too onerous for him. It became rapidly apparent that the focus of the opposition to Henderson was the Mission Committee and Mr Kirker in particular:-

'The Mission Committee wish to point out that the objects for which the Mission is established are not being carried out by any means, and the Missionary admits also that he cannot carry them out. The Mission Committee are quite satisfied on this matter, and are of the opinion that an Assistant and Successor be appointed to present Missionary.' - (17.12.19)

Clearly now the gloves were off. The Resolution provoked immediate reaction. One letter to the Directors further enlightens us as to the dynamics behind the conflict:-

'Mr Henderson has been Missionary for 42 years and has done much good and hard work, I think any objections to Mr Henderson which may be raised are being supported by younger members of the Mission who cannot possibly know the many strenuous years of work done by him.

He is now reaching the Sunset of his Life, and one cannot expect him to work in the same way as he did, say 20 years ago .... He has perhaps shown a little slackness in matters dealing with poor relief, and I have known complaints of him not assisting fully in matters of employment. He also makes promises which I regret to say he does not fulfil. My own opinion is that Mr Henderson should be relieved of his duties as Secretary and act as Missionary only.' (M. Henderson 6.12.19)

Here we can detect the crux of the conflict: a group of younger members, dominating the Mission Committee, realising that change was necessary, and with the impatience of Youth, unwilling to wait long for it. This Post War period was after all the era of great social and political change. Much of the old order had been swept away in the holocaust of World War 1, and there was great determination, particularly amongst the Young that the mistakes of the past should not be repeated. There was also, in general, a climate in which long established Institutions were questioned.

John Henderson was after all, a Victorian Missionary getting on in years, representative of a Value System which was by now by no means universal. As Malcolm Henderson, though recognising that change was necessary, points out, the younger members could not be aware of, and possibly did not want to be aware of, the extent of Henderson's past service to the society.

In some quarters the resolution provoked outright opposition:-

'At the Annual Meeting of the Congregation held here on the 11ᵗʰ, I have been instructed to inform you that this meeting expresses their utmost confidence in the Rev John Henderson as their Minister.': (Letter from Robert Hutchison, Session Clerk).

In some cases the opposition was much more vehement:-

Re Mr Kirker's motion re Missionary.

'I trust that you will allow me to have time to set a few words before the Directors regarding the above dastardly motion. It really fell like a thunder-ball to me and I am sure to a great many subscribers as well. You see we were never consulted about the matter. I must strongly protest against the hair brained policy of Mr Kirker in taking such a step at all.

Yes Gentlemen, our Missionary is certainly getting on in years, but still his grey hairs are not grounds enough to cause his retrial just yet. No, no, he is still as active as ever.': (Letter to Directors from George Paulin).

The Directors realised that there was a major problem, but swayed by letters of support for Henderson and their awareness of the debt of gratitude owed to him by the Society, would not be rushed into precipitate action. The course of action they decided upon was to set up a Special Committee on Missionaryship to take views on all sides and decide the best way forward for the Society.

The Committee carried out a painstaking Enquiry, and eventually reported on the 10th of May 1920. It noted that:-

'No feeling adverse to the Missionary personally was expressed at interviews, and all testified to his long and faithful service on behalf of the members.' - However: *'Visitation was not overtaken, especially in the outlying districts, the reason given being the growth of the city and the advancing years of the Missionary.'*

The Committee made the following recommendations:-

'The scope of the Mission should be extended and its usefulness increased. It would be advantageous to have a full time Collector. Mr Henderson and Mr Wright both favour a deaf person as most likely to ingather funds. It would also be advantageous to have a Female Visitor who could do effective work amongst the female members.

The Secretaryship should be separate from the rest. The Missionary should carry out the rest of the work.

An Assistant Missionary should be appointed, who, under Mr Henderson, would learn the Language and would accompany Mr Henderson, and so would become efficient in about a year, and so render great assistance to the Missionary.

Advantage should be taken of Mr Henderson's offer to relinquish £100 of his Salary in respect of the relief he would obtain.'

The Directors took swift action in implementing the Recommendations. The divorcing of the Administrative function from the Missionary aspect was carried out forthwith, with the long serving William Wright placed in charge of the former and John Henderson the latter.

David Marshall, a young Veteran of the War was quickly appointed as Assistant Missionary.

These measures it was hoped, would assist in increased and more effective Visitation, more efficient Administration, and expansion of the Society. Initially the moves seem to have borne fruit, as in 1921 a new larger Hall had been found in Hamilton, Govan Branch was re-established and new branches were instituted at Clydebank (to be administered by Paisley Mission), and Dumbarton. The prestige of the Society was further enhanced by the hosting of the Congress of British Deaf and Dumb Association at the Institute. A Civic Reception was given to the Delegates by the Lord Provost.

If the Directors had hoped to stem the conflict over the position of the Missionary, they were to be disappointed, however. At the start of 1921 they received the following resolution from the Mission Committee:-

'We feel the time has now come when steps should be taken for securing the services of a Missionary thoroughly experienced in the Language and ways

of the Deaf to take over full charge of the Missionaryship. The Committee, as representing the Deaf beg to intimate to the Directors their intention of inviting gentlemen who they may consider suitable to give a Lecture and conduct Sabbath Services with a view to making a choice.'

Clearly the Mission Committee (or a Cabal within) wanted a change of Missionary immediately, having evidently lost patience in the time taken for the Assistant Missionary to become fully proficient in signing. There is more than a hint of a Deaf/Hearing split, with the almost wholly Deaf Mission Committee taking a completely different line from the predominantly Hearing Directors.

It would seem that the tactics of the Directors had been that the Assistant Missionary, once fully trained, would eventually succeed John Henderson. Now whilst having some sympathy with the Mission Committee they probably felt their position threatened. The Directors' Minutes report, rather tersely:-

'After full consideration the Directors found that they could not support the Resolution as there is meantime no Vacancy in the Missionaryship, and they asked the Secretary to inform the Mission Committee that they must not invite persons to conduct Sabbath Services as Candidates.'

However, by October 1921, the strategy of the Directors lay in tatters. It is recorded on the 10th that Mr D. Marshall resigned his position as Assistant Missionary *'Having accepted a call from St. Thomas's Church, British Guiana.'* It may be that Marshall was influenced by the ongoing controversy; at any rate he certainly seems to have put a safe distance between himself and Glasgow. The Mission Committee wasted no time in formulating a new Resolution, though one more conciliatory in tone. Perhaps some behind the scenes 'fence mending' had been carried out.

Meeting of Deaf and Dumb held 29th October; Resolution unanimously passed:-

'That a new Missionary as Colleague and Successor to the Rev John Henderson is required, and this meeting suggests to the Directors that a fully qualified Missionary and experienced Teacher of the Deaf, not under 30 years of age (Whither Youth now!) *be advertised for, and that Applicants preach before the Deaf and Dumb on trial. The Directors to be satisfied on all other points.'*

The force of this Resolution, unanimously passed, eventually won the day, for the Directors, however reluctantly, placed Adverts in National and Local Newspapers and Deaf Publications in April 1922.

CHAPTER 4

JOHN ROSS & THE HOLY GRAIL

The official Centenary of the Society in 1922 was not seen as a major occasion:- *'It is proposed in some simple way to celebrate the Event.'*

Celebrations were limited to a week of Meetings, special Religious Services, a Social Gathering, and a Dinner for the Aged and Infirm Poor.

However the Centenary Year, in response to one of the Recommendations of the Missionaryship Committee, saw a major new Initiative for the Society. In conjunction with the Glasgow Society for the Education of the Deaf and Dumb, the Society appointed Nurse A.R. Grant as After-Care Educational Supervisor. Her main duties were to visit the children who had just left the Langside School and the women and girls of the Society, with a view to assisting them medically and 'to promote their Religious and Moral Welfare.' This post, though it was to be reviewed at the end of its first year, was to prove very successful.

At the end of her first year of operation, Nurse Grant had paid 134 visits to pupils who had recently left Langside, 1,066 visits to deaf women and girls of the Society, and tendered medical assistance in 21 cases. Her area of Visitation ranged from Lanark to Kilsyth. Just as importantly, she formed a Mothers'Meeting, at which she gave talks on children's diet and care of Invalids and the Elderly.

The position of the Missionary however, remained unresolved. The Advertising Campaign had only attracted a few Candidates, none of whom had proven suitable. Henderson carried on as best he could. By late 1923, the Mission Committee were again growing impatient:- *'The obtaining of a new Missionary has become a matter of urgency.'* The Post was readvertised, but with the same barren results as before.

In January 1924, however, occurred an event of great import for the future of the Society: they were bequeathed a very large Legacy from 'The John Ross Trust': the sum of £12,000.

This new found financial security enabled the Directors to make the offer of a very generous Retiral package to their faithful servant, John Henderson:-

'His salary of £350 should be continued as a <u>Retiring Allowance</u>, but it would be necessary for Mr Henderson to place his advice and assistance for at least a year to the new Minister to be appointed.' - (10.3.24)

However the procural of a New Missionary was to be no easy task. The Country was scoured for a Successor, but to no avail. It was not until 1926, with Henderson' s health failing, that George Nicholson, a Teacher at Donaldsons School Edinburgh, in training for the Ministry, was appointed as Assistant Missionary.

Finally in 1928, Nicholson took over fully as Missionary, and Henderson was at long last able to enjoy a well deserved retirement. As the 'Grand Old Man' of the Society, however, he was to remain a familiar face at Society functions over the next few years.

Top: Grand Fancy Dress Ball, early 1930's. John Henderson, bottom centre left.
George Nicholson,bottom right.
Bottom: John Henderson kicks off the 1928 Football Season

44

One of the most important developments in Deaf affairs of the period was the movement towards a National i.e. British body, to represent the Deaf.

In 1924 Representatives from all the Scottish Societies were despatched to London for a National Conference regarding the desirability of setting up a National Institute or Association for the Deaf.

The Conference did not go well. Feathers of the Scottish Delegates were severely ruffled when one of the speakers called for an 'All England Association'. Several Scottish Representatives leapt to their feet, asking if Scotland had ceased to be a part of the British Empire.

At about this time, the first green shoots of Scottish Nationalism were beginning to stir in the Scottish Political landscape, and clearly had influenced the Society's representative, Mr W Kirker. Obviously inflamed by the gaffe at the Conference, he reported back to the Society:-

'After careful thought, I cannot see in what respect the Deaf in Scotland will benefit from this Association. A History of Scotland teaches us that they (the English) are apt to become a haughty, domineering, privileged class of Aristocrats. And to crown all 'Home Rule' may come along sooner than we expect, and before anything has been done for the Deaf in either Country. I would now suggest that Scotland should have an Association of its own on similar lines as the proposed National Institute. It could work in harmony with England, yet be quite Independent.'

Such are the suppressed passions of Nationalism, though little did Kirker suspect that it would take another 75 years for his Country to achieve a measure of Home Rule. However sentiments like these helped pave the way for the Scottish Association for the Deaf.

Prize label, Ephphatha Camera Club.

In the Twenties, the number of clubs within the Society was still proliferating. There were 2 football teams - the First Team and the Reserve Team (the First Team, Blythswood Thistle, along with the Girls Hockey Team had been using the Langside School Playing Fields; the Second team was hiring a field at Anniesland) a Bowling Club had been formed, as had a Badminton Club for girls and a Camera Club. The Camera Club, known as the Ephphatha Club, quickly achieved a membership of 50, and held its first Exhibition in February 1927.

45

There had been discussion for some time within the Society concerning the desirability of starting a Magazine, to improve internal communication and to heighten awareness of the range of the Society's activities. It was decided to proceed with this venture in September 1927.

The main issue being considered by the Committee and the Directors was the possible fulfilment of an old dream: a proper Church for the Deaf of Glasgow. The very generous Bequest from the John Ross Trust, it was thought, could now turn the dream to reality. After much agonising, it was decided to commission the Architects Burnet, Son and Dick to undertake a Feasibility Study.

By the following year, all was settled. It was decided to erect the new Church on the site of the Tenement (which was owned by the Society) adjoining the Institute. Appropriately, the new Church was to be called 'The John Ross Memorial Church', since the John Ross Memorial Fund had provided much of the funds for its erection. It was hoped to make as much use of Deaf Craftsmen as possible in the construction and fitting out of the Church.

That year, after much deliberation, the Society decided to tender its strong support to the formation of 'The Scottish Association for the Deaf': to be affiliated with the National Institute for the Deaf in London: the view of the Directors being that the new Association would give a united voice to Deaf interests, and put pressure on the Government to grant similar privileges and financial benefits as gained by the Blind in the 1920 Act.

Finally in the eventful year of 1928, the name of the Society in the Constitution was altered to 'Mission to the Adult Deaf and Dumb for Glasgow and the West of Scotland'.

1929 witnessed yet more expansion in the work of the Society, with the temporary 'Blip' of the Resignation of the After Care Supervisor being immediately overcome by the appointment of Nurse C. Macdonald as a replacement.

The main thrust of the expansion was Recreational and Social, with improvements in the Hamilton Branch being most notable. A new hall in High Patrick Street was rented for the sole use of the Branch, enabling a Reading and Recreation Room to be opened. A Secretary was appointed and a troop of Rover Scouts formed.

Regular Saturday evening Social Parlours at the Institute helped foster an increased spirit of Harmony.

Competition in the Annual Games Tournament was cut throat, no doubt enhanced by cash prizes of £5.13.0d. It attracted over 95 competitors. The Camera Club held its second Exhibition. The Hockey Club had been presented by Sir Thomas Lipton the previous year with a fine silver Trophy for use in competition amongst the hockey clubs in Scotland. The Football Club continued in successful vein by winning the British Deaf and Dumb Association Shield.

Two patrols of Boy Scouts had been formed amongst the pupils of the Langside School in 1912. It was now decided by the Society to continue scouting amongst the ex pupils by forming a troop of Rover Scouts in 1928-9.

GLASGOW AND WEST OF SCOTLAND MISSION TO DEAF AND DUMB

Rover and Ranger
ANNUAL DISPLAY

WILL BE GIVEN IN

The ROYAL INSTITUTE, 237 West Campbell Street,
GLASGOW, on

Friday,   14th March, at 7.45 p.m.
Saturday, 15th March, at 7.30 p.m.

Chairman   - - - - - - -   E. H. STANLEY CRAIG, Esq.
Commissioner in charge of Extension Companies, Mrs. R. CLELAND COURLAY
Chairman of Directors   - - - - -   J. TURNBULL, Esq.

PROGRAMME - - - 2D.
All Saints, Guides, Rovers, Rangers in uniform, HALF PRICE.

Programme, first ever Rovers and Rangers Display, March 1930

The Scouts (154th Glasgow) were able to mount their first Display in March '29, and to participate in their first Camp at Auchengillan, and also in the Prince of Wales Rally at Hampden Park. Building on this successful launch, a company of Ranger Guides was formed in 1929-30 (260th Glasgow), holding a joint Display with the Rover Scouts of both Glasgow and Hamilton (75th Lanarkshire) in March 1930, and holding their first Camp that Summer.

Building work on the new Church was well under way. To help raise funds for furnishings, a large Sale of Work was organised, raising the healthy sum of £569.

1929 also saw the Retiral of William Wright, the Secretary, who had served the Society for many years. John Henderson's replacement, George Nicholson, on his Ordination, adopted the title of 'Minister and Superintendent' rather than 'Missionary'; which may indicate an important change of emphasis in the perception of the Post at that time.

CHAPTER 5

ANNUS MIRABILIS

Norman A. Dick, Architect of the John Ross Memorial Church

The culmination of the vision of a Church for the Deaf in Glasgow was achieved by the formal Opening and Dedication of the John Ross Memorial Church on 17th January 1931.

The Church, designed by Norman A. Dick of Sir John Burnet, Sons and Dick is one of the most beautiful in Glasgow. Today, though it is now owned by Keppie Design Ltd, it is a feature of the Annual Architectural Open Day in Glasgow.

The following is a description of the new church as contained in the Souvenir Booklet of the Opening:-

'The main feature of the work is the provision of a Chapel alongside the present Institute buildings which allows the religious and social work of the Mission to proceed in a wider sense than has hitherto been possible.

The presence of the Chapel has been carefully expressed in the design of the new Façade to West Regent Street. Entering under a delicately carved doorway, one is immediately impressed by the spacious Vestibule and stair leading to the Gallery. This Vestibule, with its stone lower walls and open timber ceiling, suggests a transition from the exterior to the interior of the Building, while its Lighting effects have been achieved by the inclusion of a glazed Screen on the Chapel side. The interior of the Chapel impresses one with the balance and harmony which have been expressed in its execution. The Reredos Panel and walls of the Chancel have been built with Blaxter stone which has also been carried into the side walls and windows of the Nave. A sense of Unity has been gained by the careful application of a band of carving which runs along both side walls, enters the Chancel at a higher level, and terminates on each side of the Reredos Panel with the carved inscription - 'The eyes of all wait upon thee'. The Reredos Panel and upper walls of the Chancel are finished respectively with a rich gold cloth and gold Japanese paper. A feature of the Chancel is the sunlight glass which has been used overhead, and gives a delightful sense of sunshine; and a pronounced glow in all parts of the Chapel.

The whole is surmounted by an impressive open timber Roof, springing from moulded Corbels in the Nave walls and carved Columns in the Chancel. The entrance to the Chancel is accentuated by a Rood Beam, supporting an open Niche, which spans the entire breadth of the Chapel.

To meet the requirements of the Chapel two Pulpits have been installed, one on each side of the Chancel, and between these rise the Chancel steps leading to the Communion Table. The Communion Table, chairs and Elders' Stalls have been executed in Australian Oak, and, with the additional carving which they contain, add to the charm of the Chancel. Attention is also attracted to the carved stone Font and Light Pendants in the Chancel.

A small Gallery occupies the space over the Vestibule at the south end of the Chapel, and is reached by the stair already referred to.

An Acousticon transmitting system has been installed with Receivers in the area and Gallery of the Chapel.

The existing Board Room has been enlarged, while additional accommodation, in the form of a larger Billiard and Retiring Rooms, has been included in the Basement of the new Buildings. The Session Room and Vestry are situated in the north end of the Chapel, directly over the new Heating Chamber, which contains an electrically controlled automatic oil fuel Heating Apparatus of the latest design.'

The mastery of Architectural detail and terminology contained in this description makes one suspect that it has been penned by Norman Dick himself. Who would have known the Building better?

As states the 1931 Report:- *'The Church is unique in the History of the Deaf in its beauty. For generations to come it will stand to the glory of God, a place where whosoever will enter in shall find peace, hope and rest.'*

The 'Magazine for the Scottish Deaf', having replaced the internal magazine, gives a most evocative account of the opening Ceremony:-

Interior, John Ross Memmorial Church.

'With Civic Pomp and Churchly Dignity the John Ross Memorial Church for the Deaf was opened at the stroke of 2 pm on Saturday, 17th January, in the year of grace 1931.

"Open unto me the Gates of Righteousness". The doors swung open as Dr. Bogle, Moderator of the General Assembly of the Church of Scotland, uttered these words. Cameras clicked, the Deaf Rangers and Rovers stood stiffly at attention, their colours floating in the gentle breeze as the long and brilliant procession moved into the Church. Nature herself was smiling today!

Calvinistic Scotland frowns upon Ceremony and Display but John Knox himself would have been quieted into silence for it seemed appropriate that the Deaf Community who could not speak their praise should prepare this scene of beauty - an unspoken offering to God on high.

A golden glow suffused the Chancel, an effect produced partly by the special glass in the Roof and partly by concealed lights. The layout of the Chancel does not follow the usual Scottish lines - the Pulpits (of which there are 2) being at the sides. The Communion Table is at the back, whilst at the sides are the Elder' Stalls made of Australian Oak from which rise carved figures in an attitude of prayer. A ring of intense light played upon the Pulpit occupied by the Interpreters and upon the Communion Table. The sombre black gowns of the Ministers were relieved by the scarlet and white hoods of the Doctors of Divinity present. Every sphere seems to be represented; The Church (The Right Rev the Moderator), the City (The Lord Provost), the State (The Right Hon. James Brown, Lord High Commissioner), and the Universities (Principal Rait).

The Rev Professor R Morton of the Original Secession Church broke the hush by reading the 100th Psalm. The absence of music seemed to cast a still more solemn silence upon the worshippers. The Lord High Commissioner moved into the Pulpit. 'Thine Lord is the greatness, and the power, and the glory, and the victory and the majesty.' His staccato voice made the Old Testament lesson particularly compelling.

Then followed the Dedication of the Church, its Furnishings, Holy Table, Font, Memorial Tablet and gifts; the Moderator proceeding to each in turn, reading familiar texts followed by appropriate prayers:-

'The Church's one Foundation is Jesus Christ our Lord'.

It is difficult to divorce these words from the tune which is familiar to us all, but the Hymn was not without music. The Rev J.G. Daly's mellow voice spoke the words with such feeling as to give them new point and emphasis. Then followed the Sermon. Dr Bogle's Address was a particularly happy one. 'Go thou and do likewise' was the Text he chose, stating that Christianity was a thing of deeds not words. 'The care of the Suffering and the Weak,' said Dr Bogle, 'Had been in all ages a recognised obligation of Christian people.' He urged upon members the necessity of playing their part and doing their bit in Life.

After this, the Dedication; a silence; then the Procession left by the Chancel Doors. Thus was the John Ross Memorial Church, most beautiful of all the Churches of the Deaf, duly consecrated, a House of Worship to the Glory of God and for the comfort and inspiration of the Deaf and Dumb of his Flock. AMEN. AMEN. AMEN.'

Carving of L'Abbe de L'Epee on the communion Chair.

51

Particularly striking in the Church was the beauty of the carvings. The 'Magazine for the Scottish Deaf' of Apr-May 1931 contains the following explanation of their Symbolism:-

ENTRANCE DOOR
ALPHA:- CHRIST THE BEGINNING
OMEGA:- CHRIST AT THE END OF ALL
              THINGS
I.H.S:-   JESUS

CORBEL SUPPORTING ROOD BEAM

THE VINE
THE WHEAT AND VINE REPRESENT
OUR LORD AND THE CHURCH

MINISTER'S CHAIR

L'ABBE DE L'EPEE: A FAMOUS FRENCH
DIVINE, DEVOTED TO THE DEAF

CHANCEL WINDOWS

THE EVANGELISTS
THE ANGEL: ST. MATTHEW
THE WINGED LION: ST. MARK
THE WINGED BULL: ST. LUKE
THE EAGLE: ST. JOHN

CARVED BAND TO DADO
THE WHEAT:- THE BREAD OF LIFE

COMMUNION TABLE

THE WHEAT AND VINE
X.P: CHRIST

FONT

THE TRINITY
THE HAND: OUR HEAVENLY FATHER
THE LAMB AND BANNER: CHRIST
THE DOVE: THE HOLY GHOST

VESTIBULE SCREEN

CHRIST
THE CROWNED HEAD: THE KING OF KINGS
THE LAMP: THE LIGHT IN DARKNESS:
THE RISING SUN:
THE LIGHT OF THE WORLD

One might have thought that the opening of the new Church would have had a strong 'Bonding' effect on the membership of the Society, but not a bit of it! Clearly there still existed internal tensions. The tensions had expressed themselves in forms of complaint made about the Minister and the newly appointed Secretary, Mr. W. Greig by the Mission Committee. Underneath it all, one suspects, was the question of who should run the Society, and perhaps a feeling that Deaf members in general, and the Deaf dominated Mission Committee in particular, should have more power. The following entry in the Directors' Minutes of 10.2.31 gives one side of the story:-

'The Chairman stated that the Meeting had been called to consider certain letters received from Mr W. Kirker, clerk to the <u>alleged</u> committee of the Deaf .... it was stated that the Deaf and the Mission Committee must clearly understand that the Management of the Mission was vested in the Directors, and the Mission Committee had no right to interfere therewith, or with the Minister or Superintendent, Secretary or other members of Staff.

The Directors further expressed their profound disapproval of the action of certain members of the Mission, which was calculated to cause friction and discontent among members of the Mission who otherwise would be loyal and contented. The Directors also expressed their complete confidence in Mr Nicholson and Mr Greig and their appreciation of their work since they were appointed.'

Unfortunately, no record exists of the original letters to the Directors, or of any response by the Mission Committee, so it is unclear whether the matter was resolved.

At any rate, the Mission Committee had certainly been keeping a watchful eye on things, and generally enforcing moral standards in the preceding years as this statement on their behalf from October 1929 shows:-

'Gambling in the Institute was suppressed some time ago, and greater supervision is exercised on evenings when both sexes are present. Licensed Premises - West Campbell Street:- The Minister reported seeing the Police, who are keeping the Premises under observation.'

The opening of the Church, naturally was the great Highlight of the year, but socially the Society had been very active, holding a grand Hallowe'en Carnival:-

'Instead of October 31st, we had our Hallowe'en Night on November 1st. Instead of witches we had a strange variety of characters in all kinds of strange guises. The Hall was warm with the flow of many coloured light and everybody was in a gay mood. It was a record attendance for a Fancy Dress Carnival; there being about 350 present. The Rev George Nicholson presided. He said that there was a time for everything and this evening was a time for casting off worry and care, just as they had cast off their ordinary clothes and put on motley. Balloons and steamers then appeared and everywhere there was an air of happiness and jollity. Mr Carruthers who was responsible for the arrangement and had been working at it for weeks set the pace. He encouraged us all to be happy. He deserved the thanks of all present for the wonderful evening. Then the parade began; first the Ladies then the Men. Mrs Nicholson and Mrs Hamilton were given the difficult task of judging the prize winners, and nobly they performed their task. Their judgement was endorsed by hearty cheers for the winners, who were as follows:-

MEN
1 DICK SCOTT, WHO APPEARED AS JACK DIAMOND IN 'SHOULD JACK DIAMOND WEAR THE KILT AND WHAT A KILT IT WAS!'
2 J.C. SOUTAR DISGUISED AS A 'MAGAZINE FOR THE SCOTTISH DEAF'. IT WAS MOST ORIGINAL AND INGENIOUS
3 A. KEIR AS AN 'ITALIAN ORGAN GRINDER', COMPLETE WITH MONKEY HAD EVERY-ONE ROCKING WITH LAUGHTER
4 J. DOW DEPICTING 'FORSE'

LADIES
1 J. SCOTT AS AN ADVERTISEMENT FOR 'SELO'
2 M. MCALISTER AS 'EAT MORE FRUIT"
3 J. MCARTHUR AS A 'DUTCH GIRL'
4 TINA DOUGAL COMPLETE WITH AEROPLANE REPRESENTED 'AMY JOHNSON'

KIDDIES
1 LITTLE L. PHELAN WAS A REAL 'FAIRY'
2 LITTLE M. GOW MADE A BEAUTIFUL 'PERSIAN MAID'
2 LITTLE E. MCGUIRE WAS A LOVELY LITTLE 'BROWN PAPER PARCEL'

Prizewinners, Hallowe'en 1931

The Rovers and the Rangers had enjoyed excellent Summer Camps at Gullane and Humbie respectively, and the Scottish Olympic Club had recently been formed to prepare for the Deaf Olympic Sports to be held at Nuremberg. A Swimming Club had also recently been formed.

The Royal Institute Screen Art Club had been formed with the object of *'supplying Cinematograph entertainment to the Deaf, to whom the Cinemas do not appeal since the advent of the Talking Film.'*

At least one Cinema; the Eglinton, still continued to provide a service to the Deaf and those who thought that these new-fangled Talkies would never catch on. It was highly recommended to the readers of the 'Magazine for the Scottish Deaf':-

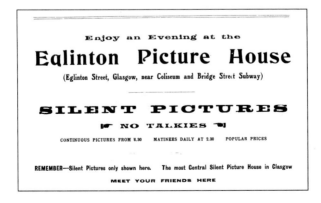

Advert Eglington Cinema, 1932

This provided temporary respite for Cinema goers, but the tidal wave of Talkies could not be held back for too long. Ironically an advance in Technology has resulted in increased disadvantage and isolation for the Deaf. However an Editorial from 'the Magazine for the Scottish Deaf' of June/July 1931 reveals an extremely prescient hope for the future for Technology for the Deaf and gives insight into the eternal problems of Deaf Communication and Education:-

'To attempt to define the word 'Education', so as to embrace the full meaning of the word in all its aspects, is no mean task. Education is a gem of many facets. In its broadest sense however, it may be described as the training of the mind, and the formation and development of character. These are its principal aims. A man of sound character and morals, who possesses mental acumen, is well equipped to be a potent factor in the life of the Community in which he lives.

Fortunately Deafness is an affliction which affects but a small percentage of the people. This is a Hearing World. Were the position to be reversed, and the incidence of Deafness amounted to a degree greatly in excess of that of Hearing, it would be interesting to observe the resultant effects, and the changes which would take place in everyday life. Such a state of affairs would be a fitting subject for a Wells Fantasy. We do not propose to follow the conjecture further, however, alluring though it seems. Enough that in reality the Deaf form a very small Minority, and as such, have to adapt themselves to the Hearing World around them.

Let us examine the matter more closely. It is evident that if the aims of Education are to be realised, the plastic Infant mind must be presented to it an infinite variety of experiences and view points. Furthermore, it must have adequate opportunity for the growth of ideas and thoughts, and the spontaneous interchange of the same. This is made possible by the use of a Currency - a medium of exchange. The medium of exchange is <u>Language</u>.

What then is the position of the Deaf? In early childhood they lack the constant auditory stimulus upon which the natural acquisition of our Mother Tongue depends. We may take it as an indisputable fact that the natural language of the Deaf is that of Gesture - not necessarily Signs, but natural demonstrative Gesture. When the Deaf infant is first confronted with our spoken Language it neither convey nor signifies anything to him. The logical conclusion therefore, is that before they can be launched up the stream of real Education, the deaf must be educated up to the standard of their Hearing brothers. In other words, they must learn a Language which at first is to them entirely new and strange, but which normal children have acquired quite unconsciously. This is a tremendous handicap with which to commence life.

The English Language is then the keystone in the Education of the Deaf; the talisman which at once accelerates their rate of learning and places within their reach the higher realms of Culture and Refinement enjoyed by their more fortunate fellows. How is this admirable end to be reached? How are Deaf children to be taught this Language? This is a problem which has exercised the minds of every Teacher, it is a Herculean task, which calls for the greatest insight and sympathy

It is a long cry back to the days of De l'Epee, Sicard, Braidwood and Gallaudet. Since the time of these pioneers, the Education of the Deaf has been carried on under steadily improving conditions, improvements in environment, apparatus and routine. Have methods and results improved accordingly? Have the Schools profited by their experiences and lessons of the past? These we consider to be very important and highly pertinent questions, and should give rise to serious thought. Even today there exist definitely opposed schools of thought upon this vital matter. Opinion is divided upon the question of Medium. There are those who firmly believe in Finger Spelling; others who are equally convinced of the value of Speech and Lip Reading; and others who think the Combined Method to be the most efficacious. It is not our province to dissect or compare these various methods; nor do we propose to comment upon them. We merely point out that a cleft exists; and it is but natural to assume from such a position that some, or many of our children are not receiving the best possible assistance in their struggle to acquire Language. That is a logical supposition. We believe that our Schools are staffed by a magnificent body of Teachers, wholehearted and sincere. It is principles we are concerned with; and our concern is that often the child is forced to adapt itself to the Method, whereas the reverse should be the case.

We think that the time has arrived for very definite research on this matter, Research based upon experience in the Classroom, Observation in Leisure Hours, Psychological Principles and Physiological Conditions. In this direction we wish to express our appreciation of the work of Dr. James Drever, the eminent Psychologist, who has given much thought to, and brought his expert Psychological knowledge to bear on the present problem. Dr. Drever brings an open, unbiased mind, and, aided by Data supplied by our enthusiastic Teachers, has already accomplished much that has provoked a great deal of speculation, and has stimulated widespread discussion.

This is an age of Miracles. Television, originally regarded as a vapouring of Scientific minds, and unlikely to become solid reality, has progressed through its experimental stages and is now an accomplished fact. The puny infant has been nurtured by its brilliant sponsors until it has developed into a robust and sturdy child.

After the Telephone - Television. The Deaf, excluded from the former, are, by a still greater stroke of genius, now able to utilise it to the full. One reads in

56

certain American cities, Television Kiosks are already installed and in full use. Deaf people are thus enabled to carry on a Telephonic conversation by means of either Lip Reading, Finger Spelling or Gesture. We look forward to the day - no doubt not far distant - when Television will be an accepted and normal factor in our daily lives.

We anticipate the following:-

HE - When can you meet me?

SHE - Oh, I'm not sure

HE - well signal me on the Radio'

Advert for ETTONE Hearing Aid

1932 was in many ways the 'Annus Mirabilis' in terms of recognition for the Society. This was the year when the Royal Institute was visited by the Deaf and Blind Helen Keller, probably the most famous Disabled person ever, and by the Duke and Duchess of York, the future King George VI and Queen Elizabeth. As an Editorial in the 'Magazine for Scottish Deaf' states:- *'It would seem that the Deaf are coming into their own, and finding at least in the public eye.'*

Helen Keller was in the Country at the invitation of the Senate of Glasgow University, who wished to confer on her the Honorary Degree of Doctor of Laws (LL.D) in June 1932.

Beforehand, at a large gathering at the Royal Institute, she was presented with her LL.D robes for the Ceremony.

Hellen Keller after receiving her Honorary LL.D Degree. She wears robes
presented by the Society. With her is Mrs Kerr Love

The occasion had an extraordinary effect on those who witnessed it:-

'We went to admire, to applaud, to appraise: we remained to worship. She calls out all that is best in one. Her radiant smile, her gentleness, her insight, her wit and humour, above all her love of Humanity, and all without the 2 major senses of Hearing and Sight could not help but force one to think what a pitiful thing most of us had made of life. More than any other person, Helen Keller

has demonstrated the Triumph of the Spirit over Matter. Chained and fettered, so that every single action is burdensome, yet she is gloriously free, soaring in heights of which most people are as yet unaware. People pity her, let them pity themselves.'

Accompanying Helen Keller were her famous Teacher, Mrs Anne Macy (Anne Sullivan), and Miss Thompson, her Companion and Interpreter.

Mr W. McKechnie, Secretary of the Scottish Board of Education paid tribute to her courage, humour and self-forgetfulness; quoting Mark Twain as stating that Napoleon and Helen Keller were the two most interesting persons of the 19th Century.

As an Educationalist, he also paid tribute to Anne Macy:-

'The emancipation of Helen Keller is one of the marvels of Educational achievement, brimful of interest and value to Miss Keller herself, and no less full of significance for Education in general. The Life of Helen Keller is one of the greatest triumphs of the Educator. It is at the same time one of the most inspiring arguments for Education that exists in the record of the Race. How many imprisoned Ariels has the World lost for want of the culture and encouragement that were needed?'

Dr. Kerr Love, a friend of over 20 years summed up the feelings of all by quoting the Poet Stedman:- *'Not thou, not thou. 'Tis us who are Blind and Deaf and Dumb.'*

When robed by Mrs Kerr Love, Helen Keller replied:-

'Dear Friends, as I stand before you in these glorious garments I feel like Judith, who, before presenting herself in the tent of Holofernes, arrayed herself in her richest attire - her bracelets, her earrings, her necklaces, her fillet of purple, her pins of gold, and her jewelled rings. So you have decked me out in splendour for the Ceremony at the University of Glasgow. Out of a very full heart I thank you.

Since I was 8 years old I have been present and taken part in many forms of exercises, and I want to say to you very sincerely that this is one of the most touching occasions I have ever attended. I could not have received a more precious token of appreciation from the Teachers and friends of those whose limitations and difficulties I share. And it makes me happy also to have Dr. and Mrs Love here, so beautifully linked with an event deeply significant in my life. For with you I hold in affection one who has long been interested in the Deaf especially, and generally in those whose handicaps multiply the difficulties of Life.

Your hands, dear Mrs Love, have adorned me with bright feathers not of my own plumage. But I will wear them as if they were mine, and hope that in Scotland fine feathers will make me a fine bird.

The warm gratitude I feel for my own Teacher makes me love all Teachers whose work is a Staff of Hope to the Deaf and the Blind. What patience, what perseverance, what ingenuity are required to open a child's mind, especially that of a Handicapped child! When I look back over the difficulties through which I have come I marvel at the sustained effort that is exerted to combat the disorganising, confusing isolating effects of Deafness. And what shall I say of the skill and devotion of those who open Doors of Opportunity for the sightless! When Teachers awaken the dormant faculties of a Deaf or Blind pupil, Prometheus like they must steal the Fires of Heaven, and with it put life into what is inert and light up a Darkness which has no end. Generations rise up and call them Blessed because they have lighted up the Lamp of Thought in many minds. When I consider how the Deaf and Blind are led out of the House of Bondage by the work of their Teachers I realise what shall some day happen to Mankind when the Highest Education is attained.

Again I thank you dear Friends.'

Even in today's cynical era, when Materialism is rampant, and Education is generally undervalued, these words still have an incredibly powerful effect, and apply just as much to the Education of the Hearing and Seeing, as well as to the Education of the Deaf and Blind.

It is interesting to note too, some of Helen Keller's answers to some of the many questions she was asked, the most revealing being perhaps the first one:-

Q - IF YOU HAD THE CHOICE OF THE RESTORATION OF YOUR SIGHT OR
    HEARING, WHICH WOULD YOU CHOOSE?
A - HEARING.

Q - WHAT PART OF THE BIBLE DO YOU LIKE BEST?
A - THE CHAPTER ON LOVE (1ST CORINTHIANS 13).

Q - CAN YOU DISTINGUISH COLOURS?
A - NO, BECAUSE THE WAVES SEEM TO TRAVEL TOO FAST FOR MY SENSE
    OF TOUCH.

Q - IF YOU GOT YOUR HEARING BACK WHAT WOULD YOU MOST LIKE
    TO HEAR?
A - MY LITTLE DOG.

Q - IF YOU GOT YOUR SIGHT BACK, WHAT WOULD YOU MOST LIKE TO SEE?
A - MY TEACHER'S FACE.

Q - IF YOU HAD JUST ONE WISH GRANTED WHAT WOULD IT BE?
A - WORLD PEACE.

Q - WHICH DO YOU LIKE BETTER, LATIN OR GREEK?
A - GREEK, BECAUSE IT IS SO MUSICAL.

Q - WHAT ARE YOUR FAVOURITE AUTHORS?
A - DICKENS, GALSWORTHY AND CONRAD.

At a grand and august Ceremony in Bute Hall, Helen Keller was conferred Doctor of Laws:-

'The spacious Bute Hall was crowded long before the appointed time, and many who arrived just before time were forced to stand. Standing space was reserved for the Students, who were on this occasion singularly quiet. The great Organ crashed as the long-robed Procession filed in, headed by the Vice Chancellor, behind whom was Compton Mackenzie, The Lord Rector. Professors of the ancient Faculty of Divinity, which takes precedence over all other Faculties, were next in their scarlet and white robes. All stood for the National Anthem, followed by the Scottish University Song:-

SAVA, SAVA, SALA, SAVA,
CORABELLA, CORABELLA.
CHING, CHING, CHINGO.
VARSITY, EGORRA! VARSITY, EGORRA.
EGORRA! EGORRA! EGORRA!!!

A prayer in Latin by Professor Fulton, Dean of the Faculty of Divinity, and then the Oration, this year from the Engineering Faculty, followed the presentation of each Honourary graduand. The Dean recited a long list of the accomplishments, the Milestones of Learning, the eminence of each, and a final burst of applause as the Recipient was capped. Country Pastors who had delved deep into the Scottish Liturgy, Ecclesiastical Legislators, Missionaries who had been exiled for long years in fevered climates and burning suns.

Then came those on whom was to be conferred the LL.D degree. They came forward in alphabetical order, a famous Italian Surgeon leading the way, each receiving the warm applause of those assembled. Half way down the list was Helen Adams Keller. Sustained and unrestrained applause was heard. Never before have I seen anything like it in that Grand Assembly. Led by Dr. Kerr Love, and accompanied by Miss Thompson her Interpreter, she went forward. For the first time too, the Vice-Chancellor left the Rostrum and came to meet her - a gracious Act of Homage to the Queen of every Heart present.

She seemed thrilled and excited. She bowed her acknowledgement, and showed plainly she was in close touch with all that passed. She knelt, was capped, and the hood slipped over her shoulders - Helen Adams Keller, Glasgow's Greatest Honourary Graduand.'

Perhaps, when reading the preceding accounts, you may yearn, however fleetingly, for the Age when we still had Heroes and Heroines.

Scarcely had the excitement of the visit of Helen Keller died down, when it was learned, at somewhat short notice, that the Duke and Duchess of York were to pay an informal visit to the Royal Institute and the John Ross Memorial Church. This was a great honour, as it was the first Royal Visit to any Scottish Mission to the Deaf.

Knowing that their V.I.P. visitors would take a keen interest in all aspects of the work of Deaf, and well aware that much of the Institute's furniture needed renewing or replacing, the Committee decided to take advantage of the occasion to arrange an Exhibition of the work of the Deaf and a Sale of Work to run from 13th October to the 15th October. The Exhibition was opened by the Marchioness of Montrose, the Hon. President of the Ladies Auxiliary, and was visited on the opening day by the Duke and Duchess of York. They were given a tour of the buildings and took great interest in all aspects of the Exhibition, stating that they were *'Gratified at the way in which the objects of the Mission were being carried out.'*

They accepted on behalf of Princess Elizabeth and Princess Margaret Rose the gift from the Society of two fireside stools, which had been crafted by members of the Women and Girls Guild. The Duke was so impressed by the general standard of workmanship, that he himself ordered an upholstered chair, the work of unemployed Deaf craftsmen.

The Duke and Duchess of York, later King George VI and Queen Elizabeth,
leaving the Royal Institute, October 1932

The sale was a great success, raising a total of £315.2.9d.

In spite of the extremely high profile of the Society, and major recognition of its efforts, all was not well nationally for the Deaf. This was a time of economic and political Crisis because of the Depression. The 'Hungry Thirties' still linger in folk memory.

A National Government had been appointed to ease the Crisis, but this meant extreme Economic Stringency. Deaf organisations had been agitating for State Aid for some time, but now all hopes seemed dashed.

An Editorial in the 'Magazine for Scottish Deaf' of June '32 bemoans the plight of the Deaf, but also points a way forward:-

'Events of great importance to our Country have been happening in rapid and bewildering succession. These events have an effect on us as individuals and also as a class. It is the latter which concerns us here. How does the present political situation affect the Deaf?

The National Government has been chosen to deal with a particular situation. It will have neither the time nor money for any matter which does not bear either directly or indirectly on the all important question of Economic Stability and National Solvency. It has no ultimate Policy; it has to deal with events as they arise. It cannot take the long and broad view: it has been specially commissioned to take a short and narrow one. Circumstances make this inevitable.

If drastic economies have been made in already existing and valuable Public Services, how can we possibly hope that those Public Services will be extended? The National Institutes for the Deaf and the Scottish Association since their inception have been standing in the Government Anterooms waiting for an audience. Once or twice they managed to get a foot over the Threshold, only to be gently but firmly pushed back and the door shut in their faces. Before the Crisis we all believed State Aid and recognition was imminent. Now we know we have been wasting time. The Exchequer is empty!

The realisation of this should throw us immediately on a new line of action. We mustn't grumble at a harassed Government. We must rethink the whole situation. Why beat our heads against a stone wall? We must profit by the Crisis. We must make the effort ourselves. When we realise this, then we can plan and carry out a new policy.

Moreover, the Crisis gives us a clue as to what the policy should be. The General Election has given us a Tariff, a Safeguarding and an Anti-Dumping Government. Industries and Agriculture most likely will be protected. Does that not indicate that whatever scheme of training we adopt, and more especially the Schemes which we all know are specially suited to the Deaf would be started and allowed to develop under favourable circumstances?

We believe the Scottish Association for the Deaf will be quick to realise its responsibility and will press for capital to commence Schemes of Work and

Training for the Deaf throughout Scotland. It is anticipated that a National Appeal will be made in its own special way for funds for this purpose. To sum up, the Crisis has put back the claim of the Deaf for State Assistance for many years, but it can give enormous impetus to Private Development, but only - if we wish and work for it.'

There seems to have been, within the Society and the Deaf Community as a whole at this time, a general realisation that the only way to ease the Employment and Economic situation of the Deaf was to institute Work and Training Schemes themselves: to indulge in their own Job Creation.

To address this very issue, the Directors of the Society evolved a Scheme to assist some of the Unemployed Deaf by issuing some of them copies of 'The Deaf World', replacing 'The Magazine for the Scottish Deaf', and edited by George Nicholson the Minister. These were to be sold on a Wage and Commission basis.

A Club for the Unemployed Deaf was also formed, meeting at the Royal Institute, both to make use of the recreation facilities, and to hold talks and lectures giving hints on gaining work. Some of the members of the Club took out an Advert in the 'Magazine for Scottish Deaf' offering their skills.

Deaf and Dumb Craftsmen

ORDERS TAKEN
FOR ANY OF THE UNDERNOTED
TRADES AT REASONABLE COSTS

UPHOLSTERY
All Renovating Work done with little inconvenience

JOINER WORK
Of All Descriptions executed

PAINTING
By Experienced Tradesmen

Let us Estimate for your Requirements

Royal Institute for the Deaf
158 WEST REGENT STREET, GLASGOW
PHONE: DOUGLAS 730

Pointing the Way

To Shoecraft

918 Pollokshaws Road

The Shop which Employs the Deaf

Advert in the 'Magazine for Scottish Deaf'   Adverts for Shoecraft Repairs,1932.

64

Some of the Unemployed Deaf were already being assisted by a venture of the Scottish Association for the Deaf. This was the 'Shoecraft Repairs' Salon in Pollokshaws Road, which employed only Deaf Workers.

Another new Initiative within the Society, no doubt stimulated by the visit of Helen Keller, was to make efforts to enable the Blind Deaf to attend religious services, and to offer them recreational facilities. By 1934, 2 Half Yearly Meetings for the Blind Deaf had been arranged.

There was, in general, more realisation of the common problems shared by the Deaf and Blind at this time; but not all agreed on common solutions:-

---

CAN THE BLIND LEAD THE DEAF?   A DEBATE

TWO WRITERS DISCUSS THE QUESTION OF

THOSE WHITE ARMLETS

A GOOD IDEA—Thinks a Hearing Man.

THE introduction of white armlets or some similar distinguishing article of wear for deaf persons, would, I think, be a good idea. Hitherto, practically nothing has been done to render deaf persons safe from traffic dangers and the many embarrassments due to their inability to hear, when on the streets and in public places.

Example of the Blind.

The use of special walking sticks—showing white in the day-time and luminous in the dark—has already proved very helpful to the blind, in that it has enabled seeing people to recognise at once their state, and to render them that consideration to which their predicament entitles them. So simple, yet efficacious, a device should soon be general in all civilised countries, and it seems logical that the application of the same principle to the deaf should follow.

Advantages to the Deaf.

One of the greatest and most poignant privations under which the deaf suffer, is that of social isolation from their fellows. The depth and scope of this condition cannot be comprehended by those unacquainted with the deaf. The white armlets would be their passport and open sesame to the friendly assistance and conversation of such of the public as were acquainteh with their language.

Moreover, it would enable them to recognise one another, and so to fraternise, where otherwise they might pass, like lonely ships in the night, not even speaking one another in the passing.

The advantage to motorists and others in charge of vehicles would also be considerable. Drivers, knowing that their audible warnings were unheard, would be more on the alert.

Public Interest.

It should also be considered that the public, through having the fact that there exists a considerable deaf population thus materially presented to their notice, would tend to take a greater interest in, and to cultivate a readiness to help them. And that is surely an end to be desired.

SHEER RUBBISH! Retorts a Deaf Man.

I AM grateful to the Editor for the opportunity of replying to the foregoing article. It is an excellent example of how a good writer, combining a little learning with a large misunderstanding, may lucubrate plausible nonsense.

Deaf Safer than Hearing.

The reason why " nothing has been done to render deaf persons safe from traffic dangers," is that nothing *can* be done that will not apply equally to hearing persons. I fail to see how white armlets will do it, unless the writer supposes they will confer on their wearers the sacrosanctity of cows in India. The simple truth is that most deaf persons are in less danger from traffic than are hearing persons, because they look-out more. How white armlets are going to save them from " embarrassments," is altogether beyond my imagination.

Fundamentally Different.

The problems of the deaf are **fundamentally different** from those of the blind. The blind person *must* call ocular attention to his condition; the deaf person neither requires nor desires to do so.

The writer comes near scoring a bull when he speaks of the isolation of the deaf. But there are considerations which he has overlooked. Those who feel their isolation most keenly are the very persons who would sooner go to the stake than wear white armlets, or do anything at all to advertise their deafness. In the born deaf, on the other hand, the sense of their isolation is much less " poignant " than is commonly supposed ; and this is natural.

Asking for Trouble.

The effect of the armlets would simply be to invite the patronage of bores and busybodies ; and any wearer pausing at a corner would be pestered by boy scouts and kind old ladies anxious to escort them across the road !

The knowledge in a motorist that a man in front of him was deaf, would not make him more alert than he ought to be in any case. It would merely give him the jumps, and might easily lead to an accident. *The deaf must take care of themselves.* If you give them white armlets, the sillier sort will simply be tempted to take risks.

In fine, the whole suggestion is sheer rubbish.

Article 'Magazine for the Scottish Deaf', June/july 1933.

Initially the Society's own efforts to stimulate Employment met with very limited success. Sales of 'The Deaf World' had clearly been disappointing, as by 1934 it had been replaced by 'The Deaf Scot' published by the Scottish Association for the Deaf; but only 2 Deaf men were employed as Canvassers.

1st Issue 'The Deaf Scot'. 1934.

Much debate was current at that time on Educational Methods. It is no surprise that the article given most prominence to in Edition 1 of 'The Deaf Scot' was 'The Plain Truth about Pure Oralism':-

'We are glad to observe that in responsible quarters the Evils of 'Pure Oralism' in Schools for Deaf children are being exposed. Consciences which have suffered long are becoming increasingly vocal. In its current issue, 'The Deaf Quarterly' of Liverpool, published from the authoritative pen of Miss B.Nevile, an article which should be in hands of every Teacher, every Parent and every person concerned in the welfare of a Deaf child - or any child. For it should be appreciated among the Public that any child may, at any time in the perilous vicissitudes of childhood's illnesses and accidents, become Deaf.

66

The Education of a Deaf child is, as it may be imagined, an exceedingly complex undertaking. There are two main methods which may be employed, that of Signs and Finger Spelling and that of Speech and Lip Reading. From these methods 3 systems have been evolved, (1) The Manual System involving the use of Signs, Finger Spelling and Writing only - a System now fallen into disuse. (2) The Combined System, which embodies the most helpful parts of both Systems: and (3) The Pure Oral System, under which Signs and Finger Spelling are rigidly banned, and all Instruction and Intercourse are conveyed by means of the visible part of Spoken Speech, sparingly supplemented by Writing.

At the present time, and for some years past, Pure Oralism has been the official method used in our Schools. It embodies a hope that is overwhelmingly attractive to a Hearing mind - or to any mind - one charged with high Idealism and the wild yearning for the Unattainable that is in all of us. The tragic pity of it is that while Hearing people get the high Idealism, the Deaf do all the wild yearning. The reader is not to suppose that we are attacking Oralism and Lip Reading, both very excellent things. We are attacking only that mistaken, and in the meantime ascendant, zeal which has arrogated to Oralism and Lip Reading the whole duty of which they can at best perform only a part.'

Miss Nevile also makes this clear:-

'No one who has any considerable experience of the Deaf, both in childhood and in adult life, is likely to deny what a tremendous uplift of a certain sort has been given to them by the teaching of Speech and Lip Reading. There is something different - not less true because not easily defined - about the Deaf Mute who as a child has made efforts to speak and lip read, from one who has not had any such instruction. In any discussion of the subject, let this be well understood and remembered.

We are concerned, however, with this question: when the years of instruction are over - when the young man and young woman are returned to their families - what is their lot? What do ordinary people think of them? How do they make and keep friendships? What of their active minds, hungry for further information? The mystery of their existence surrounds them and deepens with every passing year. Without spiritual help and contacts this mystery inescapably must darken as it deepens, closing in upon them year by year as they draw nearer to that physical dissolution upon which the starved and undisciplined imagination must dwell in increasing horror.

They received a Special Education? Yes, but no Education received in early life can provide for the normal needs of adult existence. As well might one say that having provided for the bodily growth up to the age of adolescence no more food or exercise would be necessary.

Let us consider the 2 activities by means of which the Hearing man keeps himself mentally and spiritually alive. He reads and he converses.

Only a very small percentage of those born Deaf or who have become Deaf before learning Language can read ordinary books with such understanding as would enable them to visualise from description and follow argument, and this is not from any lack of intelligence or from laziness, but for the simple reason that they do not understand the Language in which books are written. They only acquired during their years at School a small stock of English, which easily astonished and delighted their parents and friends, but which proved utterly inadequate for intelligent adult reading.

This is not the place to account for the sad failure of the Special Schools to teach the English Language to Deaf Mutes: suffice it to say that lack of devotion on the part of the individual Teacher is certainly not one of the reasons. Of the plain fact - that the great majority of the Deaf do not, because they cannot, read - there is no doubt whatever.

Next, can the Deaf converse? They were taught at School to speak and to lip read. What do these accomplishments mean for them now?

Watch the young Deaf man in a group of his social equals and it is easy to determine his position. He gets and gives nothing. If he attempts to speak conversation is checked; for his voice, if not unpleasantly harsh, is strange: and what of interest can he contribute when he has not followed what has gone before? To lip read a general conversation is a physical impossibility: for, even if every speaker spoke slowly and distinctly and every speaker's face were in a good light, how is a deaf man to know who is going to speak next? By the time he does know the remark is well on its way, the next has followed and the conversation has become unintelligible.

The Deaf man might get a considerable amount of the conversation if any friend would finger spell to him, but that inestimable boon is deliberately withheld. Throughout his School career he was taught that he must be like 'The Hearing People'. He must on no account use the Finger Alphabet, for that would make him look 'Like the Deaf and Dumb'. What he cannot get by Lip Reading he must do without. His family have for years told their friends that their son is 'Not Deaf and Dumb, but only Deaf - he speaks - he never uses Finger Spelling - he understands by Lip Reading.

On the basis of this colossal Untruth, the Deaf man was educated. He has all his life obediently pretended to be 'Like Hearing People', and in the thraldom of that effort he lives his lonely life. Sometimes a devoted mother or sister, understanding to a degree his limitations, talks to him for a few minutes every day on the commonplaces of his life, but only simple expressions can be used, and, as the best Lip Reader is constantly tripped, the Deaf man with adult intelligence soon gets tired of pretending to understand what is not after all of surpassing interest. These conversations do not last long.

Is the Deaf woman in any better case? What of the beautiful girl at the fashionable Wedding, the Restaurant, or any other social gathering? Dressed beautifully and moving gracefully, she also for a few years will bravely keep up the ghastly pretence that she is what she looks (If she keeps her mouth shut). Of human intercourse the girl gets practically nothing.

The greater the intelligence and the finer the spirit of young Deaf man and woman, the more disastrously do these artificial restrictions, arbitrarily superimposed on those which inevitably result from Deafness, operate on the happiness and fulfilment of their lives.

Miss Nevile has given us great delight by the manner in which she gently flicks the snobs who want Deaf children to be like Hearing people, and not like the Deaf and Dumb. The present position of 'Pure Oralism' in Official favour has been achieved almost solely by an appeal to that form of snobbishness - certainly human, but none the less contemptible - which is satisfied that the Deaf should look like the Hearing, and, ostrich like, assures itself that what is no longer obtrusively apparent to the eye therefore no longer exists.

Miss Nevile suggests remedies:-

'First, let the Schools be courageous enough to tell the truth to parents. Namely, that their children will never speak and lip read in such a way as to be like Hearing people, let the Schools agree most solemnly to do this. Secondly, the embargo on Finger Spelling must be lifted. The younger children in a School would need it a little, but in advanced Language teaching it would relieve an enormous amount of real stain on intelligent children but would put a stop to the unconscious Education in deceit which insistence on Lip Reading engenders. For very weariness children pretend they understand rather than be tortured further to elucidated a difficult sentence. Also it would assist the teaching of Language. Conscientious Teachers would not be tempted to use a simple sentence which they know can be lip read rather than a more involved one which they know is certain to give trouble.

Most new movements have made their way on the crest of fanatical enthusiasm and have then taken a reasonable place in the general progress. The Pure Oral System 'Making the Deaf and Dumb speak', 'Restoring them to Society' has for long enough obscured their real needs from their friends and from themselves. It is now more than time for the rationalising process to set in.'

Even today, when Deaf Education is supposedly more enlightened, much of this article strikes an uncomfortable chord.

In a survey over the Society's area of operations, the Directors ascertained that there were over 160 Unemployed Deaf. Deploring this, they decided to set up a Committee with E.H. Stanley Craig as Convenor, to draw up and set in motion schemes to provide work for experienced Deaf tradespeople, and to provide training for younger Deaf unemployed. Funds were to be raised by public subscription. Perhaps encouraged by the expansion of the Scottish Deaf Association's 'Shoecraft' Scheme, there was an air of determination to succeed in this objective.

Within a year, the Committee had made great strides. A Scheme for mattress making and repairs had been instituted. The Glasgow Society for the Education of the Deaf had donated a grant of £400, and the Society itself had added £200. Premises had been obtained at 23 Douglas Street on a 3 year lease. By 1935 the Scheme was up and running, with up to date machinery having been installed, and mattress and upholstery work being undertaken. A Tailoring Department has also been opened at Douglas Street. As well as the experienced tradespeople, seven trainers had also been taken on.

On the debit side, however, the Scheme to sell 'The Deaf Scot' had collapsed, as the magazine had ceased publication after only 4 issues.

There seems little doubt that Unemployment amongst the Deaf, as was also the case with the Hearing, was the burning issue of the day. Nationally, the Scottish Association for the Deaf, acting with the National Institute for the Deaf had lobbied Government, drawing up a proposed Deaf Persons Bill; a Clause of which sought that Vocational Training and Employment Centres for the Deaf be set up by Local Authorities.

Brochure for the Society's Douglas St. Employment Scheme, initiated 1935.

The Deaf Community, perhaps due to the severe effects of the Depression and the final advent of Universal Suffrage, seem to have been more politically aware at this period. Interest stretched beyond the Borders of Scotland and the U.K. An article published in 'The Magazine for the Scottish Deaf' in May 1932 shows that there was some demand for knowledge of other Political Systems.

J. Norman McLeod, true to the beliefs of many in that Era, gives, after a visit to the Soviet Union, a rather rose tinged view of the Communist System in Stalinist Russia; describing it as: *'The most amazing Social Experiment the World has ever seen'*. He describes the Russian Orthodox Church as *'A Religion without a Soul, based entirely on outward form and Superstition. It conspired with the Autocracy of Czardom deliberately to keep the vast Mass of the Workers in Ignorance'*.

As for the workers: *'Before the War they lived in a state of Subjugation and Misery unknown in any other European Country'*, but now they are *'The pampered darlings of the System. For them exists the whole complicated system of Ration Cards, State Holidays, State Medical Services, Sanatoria, and so on.'*

One can see the attractions of this to Middle Class Liberals and Unemployed Workers in the 30's. This, of course, was at the start of the Era of Stalin's great Purges. Hindsight reveals that the Writer must no doubt have been subjected to very effective Propaganda.

Hindsight also makes one's blood run cold at the following snippet in the September 1933 Magazine:-

STERILISATION OF THE UNFIT - NAZI'S LATEST LEGISLATION

'A law for the sterilisation of the Unfit and those afflicted with Hereditary Diseases has been drafted and will shortly receive the sanction of the Cabinet. It provides that persons such as Hereditary and Incurable Drunkards, Sexual Criminals, Lunatics, and those suffering from an Incurable Disease which would be passed on to their Offspring are to be operated upon and rendered Sterile; even against their own will, if a College of Doctors decides by a majority of votes that such an operation is necessary for the Welfare of the Nation.'

No comment on this is made in the Magazine, but one can sense the unspoken thought 'Where will all this end?' - the answer being Eugenics Experiments, the 'White Angel' and the Holocaust. What future for the Deaf in the Realm of the 'Master Race'?

CHAPTER 6

INTO DARKEST LANARKSHIRE :
EMPLOYMENT SCHEMES

The opening of the John Ross Memorial Church and the initiation of Employment Schemes seemed in many ways to herald yet another new Era for the Society. As if to underline that fact, the period around 1933-34 saw the passing of many of the old order: particularly the death of John Henderson, Missionary for 50 years, whose inspiration saw the Society expand vastly its range of activities from a base in a small rented Hall to the magnificent Royal Institute and the new church.

1934 too saw the passing of William Wright, former Secretary for 40 years; John Turnbull, Director for 24 years; Sir John Macleod, Hon Treasurer for 46 years and the Rev J Fairley Daly, Director for 13 years.

George Scott, Captain of the victorious Great Britain football team at the 1928 Amsterdam World Deaf Games.

On top of these unfortunate deaths, that year saw the Resignation of two key personnel: the Rev George Nicholson, Minister for over 8 years, and Miss C. Macdonald the Nurse Visitor. They were replaced by J. W. Greig, who took up the post of Missionary as well as his existing post as Secretary; and Nurse C. M. Thomson.

On the Social and Recreational front, 1932 saw the long awaited first Sports Gala for the Deaf at Helenvale - the culmination of 4 years of planning by the Scottish Olympic Club for the Deaf. The Gala included the following events: Men and Womens 100 Yards, High Jump, Mens 220 Yards, Mens 1 Mile, Men and Womens Obstacle Race, Tug o' War, 5 a side Football, Mens Relay Race, Girls and Boys 50 Yards and Veterans 100 Yards.

Particularly memorable were the 100 Yards Races when A. Horn won the Ladies race in the excellent time of 13.3 seconds, and George Scott (Winner of trophies in the Deaf Olympics and Captain of the Great Britain Football Team) won the Men's race in 11.3 seconds, having given his fellow competitors a start of 6 yards! The competitors, spectators and watching press declared the event a great success:- 'A most meritorious venture' (Sunday Mail), 'A decided success' (Daily Record). It was resolved to make the Gala an Annual event.

In fact the only hitch in the whole proceedings was the failure of the carefully planned system of Semaphore (or Finger Phone), due to the effects of the strong sun, necessitating a team of runners bearing the results to the Results Board. The Annual Gala paved the way for future success. The Directors' Minutes for September 1935 announced that:-

'The Missionary reported on a very successful Deaf Olympiad held in London on 17th - 24th August, at which 12 Glasgow members, including 5 competitors were present. Mr A.C. Hall won the 800m Flat Race in Record time, while both he and Mr George Scott were members of the winning British Relay Team.'

The Football Club, now known as Glasgow Deaf Athletic, had had difficulties over a number of years in obtaining a ground of their own, normally being forced simply to hire pitches, Glasgow Green being most often chosen; but in 1931, their luck turned:-

'A suitable ground had become available at Braidholme Road, Muirend, and had been secured at a seasonal rent of £8. A Grant of £10 was allowed the Club for rent and taxes, the Club to provide goal posts etc.' (Directors Minute 22.9.31).

The Club members, though had to put in great efforts to improve the pitch:-

'Messrs Beardmore and Co Ltd had granted 8 trucks of ashes for the ground, which is very sodden. Arrangements have been made for the transport of the ashes. Members of the Football Club were loading and emptying the carts.' (Directors Minute 24.11.31).

Perhaps inspired by their new home, the Club went on to win the Edwards Cup (The Scottish Deaf Football Cup) in 1933.

A Cricket Club had been formed in 1932, and 2 Swimming Clubs, Womens Badminton Club and Ladies Keep Fit Club were now operating.

This increased sporting activity reflected the general increased interest in fresh air and exercise current at the time.

Another new venture, in response to popular demand, was the formation of a Horticultural Society for the Deaf, who held their first Annual Flower show in August 1932.

Perhaps it was the interest and expertise generated by this club which influenced the choice of the Society's next venture to ease the plight of the Unemployed Deaf. The Directors had been particularly concerned at the high level of Unemployment amongst the Deaf in Lanarkshire. There were 23 Unemployed Deaf men in Lanarkshire between the ages of 16 and 25; none of whom had ever been employed. There seemed little hope of improvement in their situation. However in 1936, large gardens of the Estate of Mauldslie Castle near Crossford in the Clyde Valley, were put up for sale.

It was realised that a Horticultural Training Scheme might well meet the needs of some of the Unemployed Deaf in Lanarkshire. The property seemed very suitable: there were 9 acres of land, 12 Greenhouses, a Gardener's House and a house that could be used as a Hostel.

After long and careful deliberation, and, having sought expert Horticultural advice, the Directors decided to purchase the property in 1937. They were well aware that this ambitious Scheme would entail considerable initial and annual expenditure, but the promise of support from the Glasgow Society for the Education of the Deaf and Local Authorities; and above all the new found belief in self help for the Deaf swayed the balance. The purchase price was £2,150. The object of the Scheme was to provide sound training in all aspects of Horticulture, with a view to placements in permanent jobs at the end of the training period.

Ten Trainees were initially involved, under the care of a Head Gardener, an Under Gardener and a Cook. The Trainees received a weekly wage and were boarded in the Hostel and returned home at weekends.

The Scheme was inaugurated in March '37. Tomatoes, daffodils, tulips and chrysanthemums were grown under glass, fruit trees and bushes planted, and vegetables grown.

Trainees at Mauldslie.

74

A major contribution to the fundraising to meet the cost of running the Scheme was made by an anonymous Benefactor, who under the pseudonym 'An Unspeakable Scot', donated all profits from his book 'Wit, Wisdom and Humour' to the Scheme. Within the Society, however, it was well known that E. H. Stanley Craig, the long serving Director was the secret identity of 'Unspeakable Scot'. By 1938 over £800 had been raised.

The Society were by this time beginning to see themselves as somewhat of a 'Pressure Group' for Deaf Welfare. Concern for the plight of the Deaf in Mental Institutions had been raised with the Authorities:-

'Mr Stanley Craig reported on the meeting he and the Missionary had had with the Secretary of the Board of Control, when a sympathetic hearing was given. It was agreed to write to the Board of Control suggesting that in Institutions where there are Deaf patients, they would be under the care of warders and nurses who have knowledge of the Sign Language so that by this means of conversation, such patients might be kept mentally active.' (19.2.35)

Other business was more mundane:-

'The Church Donation Box has again been broken into, and it was resolved to take the Box from the Church.' (30.10.34)

'It was agreed to obtain from Messrs Taggarts (Glasgow) Ltd a 'Morris Eight' four door saloon with sliding roof at a cost of £142.10s, as a motor car for the Missionary.' (18.6.35)

But sometimes a special event occurred:-

'The Secretary reported on a gallant rescue made by a young member of the Mission, George Biddle, who is also a Rover Scout. On 12th March, George had jumped into the River Clyde, fully clothed, at the Broomielaw; and under difficulties rescued a woman from drowning.'

The Training Scheme for Upholstery and Tailoring at Douglas Street was running very successfully, with orders having doubled over the course of a year. This expansion necessitated the procural of larger premises in Holland Street by 1938.

The Society also took advantage of the Empire Exhibition by taking a kiosk to publicise the work of the Society and to raise funds for the Vocational Training Schemes. Articles from the workshops at Douglas Street, fresh produce from Mauldslie, the book 'Wit, Wisdom and Humour' and various other souvenirs were put on sale. Over £77 was raised.

The death of King George V in 1936 was announced in 'The Magazine for Scottish Deaf' using the words of the Official Bulletin posted on the railings of Buckingham Palace:- 'The King's Life is moving peacefully to its close. Death came peacefully to the King at 11.55.' In the Eulogy he was hailed as 'The Father of a mighty People .... we have lost a Father and a Friend.' This tragic image might have been somewhat dispelled by the knowledge that the

King's last words, as is now believed, when it was suggested to him that he might recover enough to be able to take a short trip to Bognor Regis, were, 'Bugger Bognor!'

The Society lost no time in pledging their allegiance to the new King. However they were in for a nasty shock:-

'It was agreed to send a message of Loyalty to H.M. King Edward VIII, and to crave that he continue the Royal Patronage granted to the Mission, and also that his permission be given for the use of the word 'Royal' in reference to the Institute.' (Directors Minute, 23.6.36)

'A letter dated 7.10.36 from the Keeper of the Privy Purse, Buckingham Palace was read to the Meeting stating that His Majesty King Edward VIII regretted that he was unable to give his Patronage to the Mission. It was further agreed to ask His Grace the Duke of Montrose to make further representations to His Majesty on behalf of the Mission.' (20.10.36)

This rather petulant refusal was indicative of the deep personal turmoil the new King was experiencing at the time, and no doubt of his anger that the Establishment refused to recognise the Love of his Life. Of the ensuing Royal Scandal, culminating in the Abdication of the uncrowned Edward VIII, due to his refusal to leave his Divorcee lover Wallis Simpson; no reference is made in the Society's records: reflecting the National embarrassment of the time.

However his successor George VI is greeted almost as an old friend. The 'Deaf Herald' a free magazine published by the Society to replace the 'Magazine for the Scottish Deaf', notes that *'Our people have a special interest in this Royal Pair. When the Duke and Duchess of York visited the Institute in 1932, no one dreamed that a future King and Queen were in our midst. Those who were privileged to meet them recall the kindly interest of King George VI and the charm and graciousness of Queen Elizabeth.'*

To commemorate the happy event of the Coronation in 1937, a special outing to Ayr was organised; with a grant of 2/6d being provided for Unemployed members. Meanwhile the Mauldslie Castle scheme was thriving. A list of sales for the year ending 31st March 1938 illustrates the extraordinary range of produce grown:

QUANTITY		VALUE	
97	LBS APPLES	£	1. 0. 9d
53	LBS BEANS	£	0.10. 3d
	BEETROOT	£	0.17.10d
54	LBS BLACKCURRANTS	£	1.15 0d
208	LBS BLACK GRAPES	£	11.12. 8d
168	LBS BRUSSELS SPROUTS	£	2. 0. 2d
848	CABBAGES	£	10.16. 4d
	CARROTS	£	0. 6. 0d
278	CAULIFLOWERS	£	3. 4. 5d
58	LBS CHERRIES	£	1. 1. 3d

73	CUCUMBERS	£	1.12. 7d
	CUT FLOWERS	£	13. 1. 0d
	CUTTINGS, PLANTS, ROOTS	£	26. 0. 6d
162	LBS GOOSEBERRIES	£	2. 1. 4d
	LEEKS	£	1. 8. 9d
	LETTUCE	£	6.17. 8d
23	MARROWS	£	0. 9. 7d
	PARSNIP	£	0. 3. 0d
325	LBS PEAS	£	2.19. 2d
	PEACHES	£	1.19. 8d
122	STONES POTATOES	£	3.15. 1d
124	LBS RASPS	£	2. 6. 3d
400	LBS REDCURRANTS	£	6. 6.11d
59	STONES RHUBARB	£	2.15. 0d
81	LBS STAWBERRIES	£	3. 2 . 1d
966	LBS TOMATOES	£	25. 7 . 0d
510	LBS TURNIP	£	2.19. 2d

TOTAL £ 136. 9 . 5d

The following Directors Minute shows that the perennial controversy over teaching methods for Deaf children remained, but that meantime the Society was prepared to lower its aims:-

'The Research Section of the Education Department has been asked to make enquiry into the possibility of teaching Finger Spelling to Deaf children before leaving School.' (21.2.39)

The growing clouds of War were soon to envelop the Society. The Large Hall of the Institute was requisitioned in March 1940. Blackout Regulations forced curtailment of services and much of the Winter social programme. Profits from the Upholstery and Tailoring Training Scheme were adversely affected, so much so that by 1941 the closure of the Scheme was forced on the Society.

Undaunted by this, the Society gave what assistance it could to the War Effort. The Rover Scouts were given talks on First Aid and the A.R.P., and they set up a system of Work Parties to pick sphagnum moss, used in bandages by the Red Cross. The Ladies Auxiliaries in both Hamilton and Glasgow formed a Red Cross working party; taking the place of the usual meetings. The Work Parties made articles for the Red Cross, St. Andrew's Ambulance Association and some Military Units. A War Comforts Fund was set up to send gifts to serving troops of Deaf parents. In spite of their handicap, Deaf men of Military Age did have to register for Military Service; but Certificates signed by Society officials were accepted as evidence of Deafness, and only then were they given exemption from Military Service.

After the unfortunate experiences of some Deaf people in the early days of the war, when fear of 'Fifth Columnists' and general Xenophobia were at their height, during which period some unfortunates were temporarily incarcerated; their lack of Language being interpreted by the 'Captain Mainwarings' of the time as a sure sign that they were Nazi spies; Deaf people were obliged to carry a Supplementary Card with their Identity Cards. This testified to their Deafness, and gave information on how to reach an Interpreter in the event of an Emergency.

In spite of the adverse effect of the War on most areas of the Society's activities, (even the publication of 'The Deaf Herald' had to be suspended due to lack of staff) at least by 1942 most of the Deaf of working age were now employed, taking the places of those in the Forces, and carrying out valuable War work.

As at the latter end of World War 1, there was concern as to the Employment situation for the Deaf after the War. This concern for the Future and perhaps confidence in ultimate Victory, encouraged the Directors to set up a Committee under Stanley Craig to draw up plans to deal with the expected Post War return of the spectre of Deaf Unemployment.

Society Appeal, 1940's; illustrating the wide range of services provided by the Society, as well as the problems encountered by Deaf people.

It may be that some of the confidence in ultimate Victory was due to the receding fears of Invasion and the Intervention of the United States and the Soviet Union in the War. At any rate, new found Solidarity for the Soviet People inspired the Society to set up a fund for Deaf children in the Soviet Union. Over £100 was collected by George Scott and this was sent to Ivan Maisky, the Soviet Ambassador.

The 'Dig for Victory' and 'Land Army' Campaigns, reflecting the need for the Country to be self sufficient in food, fortunately made the Mauldslie Castle Scheme untouchable, in fact by 1944; it was set to expand. A sum of £1,600 had been earmarked for increased Hostel accommodation in order to take on more trainees. Word of the success of the Scheme had spread, and enquiries had been received from other Local Authority areas concerning placements of Deaf trainees. Since 1942, the workforce at Mauldslie, at the society's request, had been assisted by members of the 'Women's Land Army', hence increasing the production.

A 'Land Girl' at work: Mauldslie, World War II

Happily also for the Society, James W. Greig the Missionary, was successfully ordained to the Ministry in 1943, enabling him to carry out Communion, Baptisms, Weddings and Funerals. Additionally his Wife Doris formed a Girls Association for those between the ages of 16 and 35, with regular weekly meetings.

Meantime the Employment Committee had not been idle. To emphasise the potential injustice of widespread Post War Unemployment amongst the deaf, a summary was made of the huge range of skills of Deaf workers employed in 1944.

This was contrasted with the Unemployment Rate of 41% amongst the Deaf in 1938/9.

MEN.

Occupations.	No. Employed
Engineering.	
Brassfinishers	3
Blacksmiths	2
Boilermaker	1
Coremakers	2
Caulkers	2
Drillers	2
Engravers	5
Fitters	11
Hammermen	2
Hydraulic Riveter	1
Instrumentmakers	3
Metal Polishers	25
Machinists	5
Galvaniser	1
Paint Sprayer	1
Riveters	2
Tracer	1
Turners	3
Ventilating	1
Welder	1
	— 74
Boot and Shoe repairers and makers	52
Woodworkers.	
Boxmakers	2
Chairmakers	3
Joiners and Cabinetmkrs	17
Ships Joiners	5
Sawyer	1
Patternmaker	1
	— 29
Printing Trade.	
Bookbinders	9
Artists	2
Compositors	2
Cutters	1
Litho Artists	5
Paper Cutter	1
	— 21
Other Occupations.	
Bakers	9
Barber	1
Beltmaker	1
Brushmakers (blind)	6
Bus Inspector	1
Cartwrights	2
Clerks	3
Coalmen	5
Coachpainters	2
Dairymen	5
Designer	1
Carry forward	36 176

MEN—continued.

Occupations.	No. Employed
Brot forward	36 176
Dental Mechanics	4
Dustmen	3
Electricians	2
Football Stitchers and Saddler	5
Forester	1
French polishers	8
Gardeners	17
Garage hands	2
Golf Club Maker	1
Glass Workers	2
Ham Curer	1
Hotel and Hospital Handymen	3
Kiln Setter	1
Locksmith	1
Motor Van Drivers	2
Painters	9
Presser	1
Rubber Workers	9
Schoolmaster	1
Stockkeeper	1
Stokers and Firemen	5
Stone Cutters	4
Stablemen	2
Tailors	7
Timekeeper	1
Tinsmiths	2
Umbrellamaker	1
Warehousemen	2
Upholsterers	18
Weighing machine Maker	1
Wood Engraver	1
	— 154
Labourers.	
Bakers	13
Brickworkers	5
Builders	2
Dock	2
Engineers	10
Farm and Garden	14
General	23
Iron and Steel Works	12
Joiners	4
Pithead	1
Shipyard	9
Sand Quarry	2
	— 104
TOTAL OF MEN	**434**

WOMEN.

Occupations.	No. Employed
Boxmakers	2
Clerkesses	2
Cook	1
Collector	1
Domestics	36
Dressmakers and Tailoresses	33
Dairyworkers	2
Engraver	1
French Polishers	3
Farm Worker	1
Garage Hands	3
Carry forward	85

WOMEN—continued.

Occupations.	No. Employed
Brot forward	85
Handcrafts	2
Hosiery Machinists	2
Laundry Workers	4
Packers	7
Paint Sprayers	3
Patternbook Makers	2
Rubber Worker	1
Tool Workers	2
Tracer	1
Upholsterer	1
TOTAL OF WOMEN	**110**

Post-War Employment.—The severe unemployment among the Deaf and Dumb which persisted for so many years after the War of 1914-18 is a tragedy which the Directors are anxious should not be repeated when the present hostilities cease. A special committee is examining this problem.

The facts given below will be of interest in regard to employment:—

1. Area served by the Mission—Glasgow, Lanarkshire, Dunbartonshire, and part of Argyllshire.
2. Number of Deaf and Dumb (not in institutions) in the area—

Males	...	526
Females—Single	...	188
Married	...	283
Widowed	...	45
		— 516
		1,042

3. Age Distribution—

	Glasgow Males	Glasgow S	Glasgow M	Glasgow W	Lanarkshire Males	Lanark S	Lanark M	Lanark W	Dunbartonshire Males	Dunbarton S	Dunbarton M	Dunbarton W	Argyllshire Males	Argyll S	Argyll M	Argyll W
15-19	21	10			10	8			3	1						
20-24	28	16	7		13	4			5	3						
25-29	36	8	19		16	7	6		1							
30-34	28	8	22		8	3	3		3	1						
35-39	45	17	21	1	15	3	9		1	1						
40-44	42	6	47		9	4	7		3	3						
45-64	152	40	95	18	30	16	27		5	3	2	1				
65 & over	23	7	7	13	19	3	7		3	2						
Total	375	114	218	34	128	49	52	10	16	14	3	1	7	11	4	
Single Women		114				49				14				11		
Married Women			218				58				3				3	
Widowed				34				10				1				

Glasgow	741
Lanarkshire	245
Dunbartonshire	34
Argyllshire	22
TOTAL	**1,042**

4. Number of Deaf and Dumb children leaving school each year, and becoming available for employment—average 15.
5. Numbers employed in 1938/39 :—

MALES—				
16-20	...	...	...	8
21-30	...	...	...	28
31-40	...	...	...	42
41-50	...	...	...	35
51-65	...	...	...	17
				— 128

The Employment Committee also scented some benefit for the Deaf in the Disabled Persons (Employment) Act of 1944. Though this was primarily intended for the benefit of Ex-Servicemen and Women, it was seen as being potentially helpful to the needs of the Deaf: especially so since Mr Tomlinson, the Chief Architect of the Act, stated at a conference of Deaf Societies:-

'I do not think there is any Section of the Disabled in the Community that has been more imposed upon than the Deaf. I do not know any affliction that is more difficult to bear. As I see it, at any rate, Deafness has in it the possibilities of more disturbance than any other of the common Disabilities, and anything we can do to overcome the Disability should be done.'

Part of the key to solving the problem of Deaf Unemployment was seen as Education. The Committee realised that a higher standard of Educational Achievement was necessary for the Deaf to compete with the Hearing in the quest for Employment, therefore a special Education Committee was set up to liase with the Scottish Education Department.

By late 1944, due to the Invasion of Europe, the hint of Victory was in the air, and the lifting of Blackout Restrictions enabled many evening meetings to be resumed over the Winter Session.

Ultimate Victory in 1945 saw Thanksgiving Services on V.E. day and V.J. day. It is noticeable that the dip in Church attendances following World War 1 was not replicated at the end of World War 2. Possibly this reflects the National mood of Optimism: 'A Land Fit for Heroes', and the promise of the new Welfare State - in contrast to the despair and disillusionment after the First World War. The Directors were able to appoint a new full time Missionary, Osborne L. White (to be replaced by J. Stewart Lochrie within 18 months) to Hamilton Branch, as well as procuring new, more spacious accommodation in Union Street, Hamilton. A Furnishing Fund was initiated, and various Flag Days and Sales of Work were held to this end; one of these being opened by Sir Harry Lauder.

The last vestiges of War Restrictions on the Society, apart from general Rationing, vanished with the Derequisition of the Large Hall in November 1945.

In general, after the Austerity of the War, expansion and new Schemes were in the air. At Mauldslie, in addition to the extension of the Trainees' Hostel, new greenhouses were built and a tractor purchased. Even a Bowling Green and a new Recreation Hall were now provided. Much of this was made possible by the publishing of a new book 'Morals, Maxims and Musing' by 'An Unspeakable Scot'; bringing the total raised by him to a truly astonishing £9,500.

1945 also marked the 50th Anniversary of the opening of the Royal Institute. After much consideration of how best to celebrate this Jubilee, it was proposed to start a fund for an Eventide Home. There had been much general awareness of the isolation of the Elderly Deaf, and it was felt that assistance to this relatively neglected section of the Deaf Community was long overdue. The following Appeal was launched:-

APPEAL FOR

£25,000

to establish an

EVENTIDE HOME

for the
**Aged and Infirm Deaf and Dumb
of Glasgow and the West of Scotland**

THIS IS AN URGENT NECESSITY

Many aged Deaf and Dumb live alone with no one to talk to, no one to care for them in sickness or infirmity. They are denied many of the pleasures of the hearing world— wireless, concerts, films, etc.

Will you help ?

Donations may be sent to—
The Chairman - E. H. Stanley Craig, Esq. C.A.
128 Hope Street, Glasgow, C.2
The Hon. Treasurer — Lt.-Col. Norman MacLeod, C.M.G., D.S.O.
149 West George Street, Glasgow, C.2
or
To the Secretary - - Rev. James W. Greig
158 West Regent Street, Glasgow, C.2

CHAPTER 7

POST WORLD WAR II BLUES

The appeal achieved very promising initial results. Various properties were inspected, and eventually a large house in Roman Road, Bearsden was purchased in October 1947. Purchase was possible through contributions from the Appeal Fund and grants from the General Fund, The John Ross Memorial Fund and The Sir Thomas Lipton Trust Fund. The Committee were of the opinion that the Home could be maintained by payments received from residents for board and lodgings, grants from Local Authorities and Assistance Boards, and public subscriptions. However problems were soon encountered, fundraising for 1948 proved disappointing *'Possibly owing to the misunderstanding regarding the Mission's position under the National Health Services.'*

One can well understand that the general Public may have considered that the new National Health Service would take care of all 'From the Cradle to the Grave.' The Directors of the Society now realised that in this new Era of Political and Social change, it was an urgent necessity for the Society to redefine itself and work out its relationship with the National and Local Authorities.

An Editorial in the 1949 Annual Report illustrates the problems:-

'As some confusion may exist as to the position of the Mission under the National Health Services, it has to be emphasised that The Mission is not 'Nationalised', nor is there any possibility of it being 'Taken over'. The National Assistance Act (1948) states that the Local Authorities may make provision for the welfare of the Deaf and Dumb; that they may employ as their Agents the existing Welfare Societies; and that, in return, they may make a contribution to the funds of these Societies. The Local Authorities concerned have been invited to make use of the Welfare Services of the Mission, but negotiations have not been completed. It should be clearly understood, however, that any financial assistance which may be received from Local Authorities must be applied to the further development of the work of the Mission. Support from the Public is, and will be, necessary, and the Mission is registered for this purpose under the National Assistance Act to continue receiving subscriptions and raising funds.'

Recognising these difficulties, it was decided that yet again it was necessary to increase public knowledge of the work of the Society, and to this end a programme of lectures was carried out by the Rev Greig, Mrs Greig and Nurse Thomson the Nurse Visitor.

The potential benefits of cooperation under new Legislation were vast. The Society was already benefiting slightly from the Disabled Persons Employment Act - a few trainees at Mauldslie were employed under the Act, a proportion of their wages being paid by the Ministry of Labour. The majority of Deaf of working age were by now registered under the Act.

Offset against this was the curtailment of the activities of the Church Benefit Insurance Society. Due to new Legislation, it had to register as a Voluntary Benefit Society; somewhat reducing its benefit to the Deaf Community.

Despite the uncertainty, it was decided to proceed with the fitting out of the Eventide Home, and on 6th September 1949 'Craigholme' was officially opened by the Lord Provost of Glasgow, Victor D. Warren. Initially Craigholme housed 13 residents, with potential to take up to 24. Staff consisted of a Matron, Assistant Matron and a Gardener/Handyman.

Brochure, Craigholme.

Some of the shortfall in funds was covered by the 'Unspeakable Scot' fund, which had now raised the total of £20,528 since its inception. Stanley Craig had now become Chairman of the Society, succeeding Donald Dewar, who died in 1946; and this, coupled with his extensive 'Incognito' work on behalf of the Society resulted in the grateful Society naming the Eventide Home after him at the suggestion of the Deaf members.

The period around the opening of Craigholme should have been a time of celebration for the Society, and publicly, for the members in general, perhaps it was. However there were severe internal problems.

The Annual Report for 1949 makes no mention of the problems; the opening of Craigholme aside, the only item of note mentioned is the rather abrupt Resignation of the Rev J. Greig to take up a post in Edinburgh formerly filled by his father, and his subsequent, rather swift replacement as Missionary by J. Stewart Lochrie, the Missionary at Hamilton.

The Directors Minutes for 1949 are more illuminating however. On 30th April 1949, the Secretary, George Wallace resigned to take up an appointment as Deputy Superintendent of Leeds Deaf and Dumb Society. George Wallace had only officially served as Secretary since February '49, before that he had served as Cashier/Bookkeeper since May '46. The Rev Greig had served as Minister and Secretary since the previous Secretary Mr J. Barton Potts had been asked to resign by the Finance Committee as he had not prepared Financial Statements for the Annual Meeting in May '46.

A very short time after Wallace's resignation, the Rev J. Greig departed, and on 14th June, Stewart Lochrie was appointed as over all Missionary. Around this time, whether before or after the resignations is unclear, it had become apparent that financial irregularities existed. What is certain is that Auditors were called in on 5th July. Meanwhile, a new Secretary, Mr Leslie had been appointed on the 24th May. His area of responsibility, and that of Stewart Lochrie was quickly determined:-

'It was decided that Mr Lochrie should have full charge of the Ministerial work of the Mission, and at the same time supervisory charge of the Clerical Staff, of which Mr Leslie would have full charge, but it was to be understood that Mr Lochrie was to be in control.' (20.6.49)

The Auditors realised almost immediately that the scale of the problems was much greater than had been anticipated. It was quickly ascertained that no P.A.Y.E. returns had been made for Mauldslie Employees, and that the Glasgow Collections had not been properly declared. It was decided to contact the former Secretary, George Wallace, and the Rev Greig for an explanation:-

'Mr Craig reported that the position regarding cash deficiencies was not much clearer as no great help had been obtained from Mr Wallace's reply to the letters from the Secretary. It was decided to ask Mr Wallace and Mr Greig for an explanation and to ask the Auditors to review the position at an early date.' (5.7.49)

When the Auditors produced their interim Report, it was somewhat of a bombshell. Mr Brown of the Hon Treasurers Office, and 2 Auditors reported to the Directors that:-

'He had received 2 Savings Bank Accounts from the Secretary which had operated in the name of the Rev. James W. Greig. He (Mr Brown) further stated that he had no previous knowledge of the existence of these Accounts, nor had he any record of the purpose for which various withdrawals had been made.'

On the face of it, this seems very damning indeed, but it must be pointed out that we are not hearing the Rev. Greig's side of the story, if indeed it was ever given. We also must ask ourselves the question, if these Savings Bank Accounts were 'Black Accounts' kept secret for the purpose of misappropriation of funds, then how did they come into Leslie's possession? Had the Rev Greig passed them over to him on his departure as an admission of guilt, unable to face financial inquisition, but wishing for the truth to be revealed in a roundabout way?

Or could it be that Wallace had been the villain of the piece and had encouraged the Minister to open the accounts, and had made withdrawals by means of forged signatures? Or had they both formed a Cabal?

The last possibility that exists was that there never was any financial wrongdoing, only colossal financial incompetence on all sides; and that the purpose of the accounts was entirely innocent.

Further developments may indicate that there was indeed some truth in this:-

'The Secretary (Mr Leslie) reported that he had written 2 letters to Mr Wallace, and 1 to Mr Greig on the subject of discrepancies discovered by him. Mr Greig had replied stating that there had been a deficit in Mauldslie Accounts at the change over (i.e. when he became Secretary in 1946) and on other matters of monies received and not entered, this was a matter of Mr Wallace only. Mr Wallace had replied to the first letter giving the same reasons for the alleged Mauldslie shortage, but had ignored the second letter sent to him by the Secretary. Mr Craig pointed out that the alleged Mauldslie shortage was due to a double entry on the credit side and that the alleged cash shortage did not exist. Mr Belch (Auditor) stated that his Assistants had been working on the Savings Bank Accounts and the Treasurer's Books. The Treasurer's Books were in perfect order, but the Savings Bank and other Accounts were a very complicated business and would take some time. He preferred not to make any definite statements at this time.' (30.8.49)

Whether there were any cash deficiencies at Mauldslie, the investigation had certainly opened a financial can of worms. Mr Craig's explanation seems a bit too pat, ignoring the question of the P.A.Y.E. returns and the deficiencies alleged by Greig and Wallace as far back as 1946 (Though their allegations beg the question: why did they not take action then?). One must also bear in mind the fact that Mauldslie was Stanley Craig's 'Baby', so he would be rather reluctant to have a shadow cast over the Project.

A subsequent Auditors' Report further reveals that financial incompetence there most certainly was. Mr Ker of the Auditors stated to the Directors that:-

'His Staff had found the books to be in a most deplorable state, and that many errors occurred both on the credit side and the debit side. It would be impossible to assess the exact amount involved, and that the best plan would be

to forget the past and start a fresh system of Book keeping as soon as possible.' (27.11.49)

It seems then, that the truth behind this whole sorry episode did not come out at the time, and is no more apparent to us now than it was then. If it did then it was 'Airbrushed out of History'. That there was gross financial mis-management is certain, whether the chaos in the Financial Records was used as a smokescreen to mask misappropriations of funds cannot be proven - no jury could convict either or both of the Dramatis Personae on the available evidence, though if wrongdoing took place, it is hard to believe that the Rev Greig was solely guilty, or that Wallace was entirely innocent.

Or it may be that no crimes took place; only incompetence over a long period of time. It is extremely regrettable in particular that no firm conclusions on the question of the Savings Bank Accounts are mentioned, if indeed they were arrived at, so doubt must remain.

The Scandal was hushed up, though some whispers, casting suspicion, very possibly unjustly, on one or the other penetrated to some ordinary members. The system of accounts was set to 'Year Zero', as suggested and eyes were determinedly focused on the Future, away from the murky waters of the Past.

The new post of Book Keeper/Cashier had already been advertised. The present Clerical Staff would be intrigued to know that the Auditors, in true Sexist vein, and ignoring recent events, recommended that:- 'If possible preference to be given to a Male.' Women, no doubt, were seen as incapable of doing hard sums. The new Secretary, Mr Leslie, did not last long in his post. Perhaps overwhelmed by the sheer scale of his task, or simply not up to the job, he resigned at the end of November 1949, leaving the books in a 'Very unsatisfactory state'.

The whole Affair fizzled out on somewhat of an ironical note:- Leslie, the man who had first detected alleged cash deficiencies had proved to be not particularly financially competent himself; and the final recommendation of the Hon Treasurer was that all cash should be in the charge of Miss Cochrane of the Office Staff, and that she should have the only key to the Safe!

By January 1950, Stewart Lochrie was appointed as temporary Secretary, the burden of his Missionary work having been eased somewhat by the appointment of William Gemmell as Assistant Missionary.

There remained financial concerns however. Clearly there had been some internal debate over the drain on the Society's finances of the Mauldslie Scheme. A short excerpt in the 1950 Report reminds readers that:- *'From a financial point of view, this Nursery cannot readily be compared with a Commercial Nursery since it is not feasible to employ the Trainees on a Seasonal basis .... they remain the Year round, paid the full rate laid down by the Agricultural Wages Board.'*

In 1951, it was deplored that: *'Some Local Authorities have discontinued their support towards the Scheme since the introduction of the National Assistance Act in 1948.'* There was a recorded deficit of £1,900 for the scheme for 1950 so one can understand the concern.

The Rev Stewart Lochrie (He was Ordained in April 1951) set about his work with enthusiasm. He articulated the problems of the Deaf in a very Modern, up to the minute way: making use of the 'Buzz Words' of the day, and relating them to the Deaf experience. His eloquent introduction to the 1953 Report is a good example of his approach:-

'In this era of man's advancement in the field of Scientific Discovery, the Public are constantly being presented with new words, such as Atomic Fission, Neutrons and Cyclons. In the field of Aeronautics we have now come to under-stand a new term 'The Sound Barrier'. While it is true to say that this is a problem which is comparatively new to the Scientists of the Aeronautics field, the Sound Barrier had been in another sense the greatest problem which the Deaf have had to face since Time Immemorial. The 'Barrier' has prevented them from being able to enjoy the companionship of the World of Sound, has shut them out of the World of Music, of the Theatre, of Culture, and has allowed them only a modified form of Education. Even the opportunity of Spiritual Guidance and participation in Public Worship may be denied them by this 'Sound Barrier'.

The Mission's objects are set out clearly elsewhere in this Booklet, and if you study them closely, you will find that our aim, like that of the Aeronaut, is to break down the Barrier of Sound, where that is possible, to give the Deaf the opportunity of Companionship, Worship, Recreation, Social Education, Employment, and to live as full a Life as possible.'

It is clear that he regarded the Annual Report much more as a Public Document, and hence an opportunity to reach 'Hearts and Minds' of any reader; and also perhaps wallets. At all stages, he always seemed to be on a mission to explain.

An immediate innovation was terming the Y.M. and Y.W.C.A. as the 'Youth Fellowship'. A new Drama Club had also been formed in 1953. It was around this period when references to the Temperance Society cease, and it may be implied that it either disbanded or simply withered away. Perhaps Temperance; one of the Pillars of the Society in former days, was now becoming unfashion-able. Television sets had been installed at the thriving Hamilton Branch and at Craigholme, where it was much appreciated by the residents.

It was noted in the 1953 Report that although Branches still existed at Dumbarton and Coatbridge, numbers were small: one of the problems being that many of the Deaf in these areas preferred to go to either Glasgow or Hamilton *'Where they have the opportunity of meeting with a greater number of the Deaf.'* This factor was largely instrumental in the disbandment of the Coatbridge Branch by 1960.

It was fortunate that Stewart Lochrie had taken to his new duties so ably, as in 1955 the Society lost one of its ablest ever Chairmen and fundraisers due to the death of Stanley Craig; now publicly revealed as the 'Unspeakable Scot.'

In his Obituary he is described as:- *'........ A Fairy Godmother who helped when things looked impossible and who made Mauldslie his fulltime work.'* A Quotation from Abraham Lincoln, already used in one of his books, is given as his Epitaph: *'Die when I may, I want it said of me, by those who knew me best that I always plucked a thistle, and planted a flower where I thought a flower would grow.'*

He was succeeded as Chairman by Ex-Provost James Mincher. The 'Unspeakable Scot' Fund, however carried on after his death, and William Archibald took over as Convenor of the Mauldslie Scheme. Another personnel change was the replacement of Nurse Thomson (who retired due to ill health) by Nurse C. M. Steen as Welfare Supervisor.

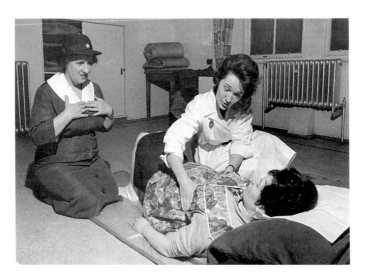

Nurse Steen in action; assisting in breathing Exercises, Royal Maternity Hospital , Glasgow.

The unfortunate adverse effect on fundraising by the advent of the Welfare State still continued to be a problem in the mid 50's. The 1956 Report bemoans:- *'There is today a very definite change of attitude towards those who are in need. People are included to shrink their responsibilities by making pronouncements concerning the Welfare State and its duties towards those in hardship.'*

However the Society was not content to simply complain about its lot; an innovatory method of fundraising was harnessed by utilising the B.B.C. Radio Weekly Appeal. Stewart Lochrie successfully raised £327 from the Programme: clearly reaching a mass audience was potentially very rewarding for the Society.

In spite of this, problems of finance reached crisis point in 1957, forcing the Directors into making cuts in services. The axe eventually fell on the Mauldslie Scheme. However the 56-57 Report states that the reason for closure *'Is primarily a happy one: the lack of boys who require such training.'*

There was truth in this:- The mid and late 50's were an era of high Employment. In Lanarkshire the Steel Works were expanding and taking on lots of workers. There was an effective scheme for placing the Deaf in Industry, and Schemes for the Deaf remained at Fairyhill Nurseries, Kilmarnock, and Shoecraft Repairs in Glasgow.

Leaflet for Employers to encourage the placement of Deaf workers in Industry, 1950's.

But it is evident that the overriding reason for closure was financial: the drain on the Society's resources was too great. As the 1958 Report records:- *'This has been one of the most difficult years our Mission has experienced, and that we have managed to weather the financial storms is in no small way the result of our many friends from all walks of life who have contributed to our cause.'* Winding up the scheme, with the potential realisation of a large sum from the sale of the land, it was hoped would set the Society back on the financial rails. This hope influenced the decision in 1959 to proceed with a much needed extension to Craigholme, providing 10 extra beds.

At least the Directors could console themselves with the fact that the public profile of the Society was again very high due to the first Televised Service from the John Ross Memorial Church:- *'When through the medium of Television our beautiful Church was shown to millions of people. Here at last we were able to show what we have tried to describe in words. The reaction of the General Public was most heartening.'*

Stewart Lochrie, in fact, seemed to have mastered the medium; proving popular with Hearing as well as Deaf audiences; so much so that he was asked to conduct a Televised Easter Service using the Combined Systems of Speaking and Signing.

The Minister was also quick to realise the implications of Social Change in the Full Employment, more affluent late Fifties, and the consequent need for more Youth work. He acknowledged 'The problem of Teenagers' (As far as much of society was concerned, they did not seem to have existed before the late Fifties). He raised the profile of the Youth Fellowship to obviate the problems of 'Young Deaf people leaving the sheltered atmosphere of School life and entering the broader, sterner atmosphere of the World outside.'

By this time the Society was cooperating with the Health Service in a Programme of early detection of Deafness in children. All children of Deaf parents (though Deafness is not usually hereditary) were taken by the Welfare Supervisor to be screened by Specialists.

Screening for Deafness.

90

CHAPTER 8

OLD BATTLES REFOUGHT

Nationally the Post War Baby Boom was a ticking time bomb waiting to explode on the Employment Situation. One of the main reasons for the relatively full Employment of late 50's was the low Birth Rate during the War years. By 1960 huge numbers of young people were joining the available Labour Force, and now there were insufficient vacancies. The Society had prepared for the implications for Deaf Employment by pressurising the Education Department to provide a special Day Release Course to enable the Deaf to gain theoretical as well as practical skills. This Course was instituted at the David Dale College in October 1959.

By great effort almost all school leavers were placed in Industry and Commerce: making possible the proud boast in 1960 that the Unemployment Rate of the Deaf in the area of the Society was only 1.5%, as opposed to an average Unemployment rate of 8.5% amongst the Hearing. Mr W. Gemmell, Missioner at Hamilton was also able to place all school leavers.

Vigilance was also required in screening potential new legislation - again illustrating the conflict between new, well-intentioned general National Welfare Schemes, and the more specialist services provided by the Society. The Younghusband Report was particularly criticised:- *'The paramount need of the Deaf is the assistance of the Specialist who is not only an expert in their Language, but who intimately knows and completely understands the ramifications of Deafness. The proposed 'Welfare Assistants' and 'Officers with a general training in Social Work', however well intentioned their casework service might be, would create far more problems than they had the ability solve. Their 'Measure of skill in Communication', and lack of understanding of the Psychology of the Deaf would add to, rather than lessen the load of problems of special difficulty presently being cared for by the Professionally trained Specialist on the Mission Staff.'*

The other main strand of criticism of the Report was its implication that Societies for the Deaf tended to Isolate rather than Integrate: encouraging the Deaf to socialise with those with a similar handicap, and hence discouraging them from the company of Hearing people. As the editorial from the 1961 Report argues however:

'This line of thinking is understandable, at first glace it would seem a feasible pronouncement. Let us however, look at the situation from the point of view of one who is Deaf. Today the young Deaf person is taught to communicate by

the Oral Method, that is by Lip Reading and Speech. This is a tremendously difficult Art, which places great strain on the Lipreader. On top of this strain, is the natural desire to appear normal, so we find the Deaf person straining to catch every word, because if he doesn't he is liable to give the wrong answer and appear stupid. This is the natural fear that rests on every Deaf person. What then is more natural than that he should want to relax, to release himself from the nervous tension and strain of living in a Hearing Environment. So he goes to the one place he knows he will be accepted as one of the crowd, where he can communicate in an atmosphere of understanding, where no allowances need to be made, a Community where he is at one with the World. This then, enables the Deaf man or woman to go out into his or her World of Home, Employment, Sport or Friendships; renewed and strengthened, more able to be integrated with the Social, Economic and Spiritual Spheres of Daily Living.'

Again the importance of the continuation of the work of the Society and of Specialist Deaf Welfare workers offering a 24 hour Interpreting Service to Hospitals, Police etc is stressed.

By 1963 some sort of compromise had been reached. Students taking the new 'Younghusband' Certificate Course in Social Work at the Scottish College of Commerce, as well as those taking the Probation Officers and Child Care Study Courses were given practical instruction in Deaf Welfare by being given placements within the Society for periods of their Courses: thus giving new recruits to the above Professions an insight into the problems of the Deaf as well as awareness of the high standard of facilities that the Society had to offer.

In 1962 occurred another important milestone in the History of the Society: Amalgamation with Paisley Mission, with both Societies retaining their identities (it was hoped), but being amalgamated in every other way. This it was confidently felt would improve welfare services in the Paisley and Renfrewshire area (not least as it had been decided to buy the Paisley missioner a small car).

At Glasgow, the clubs still thrived, and indeed were further expanding. Since 1960, no doubt due to increased awareness of the needs of the elderly, an Old Age Pensioners club - 'The Regent Club' had met fortnightly at the Institute; a new Physical Training class had been formed at Northland School and there was a new Men's Club. The Drama Club had presented the pantomime 'Dick Whittington'; an interpreter making it possible for a large hearing audience to attend. Glasgow Deaf Athletic F.C. had been beaten finalists on their first entry to the British Deaf Amateur Cup, and the John Ross Badminton Club and the Carpet Bowls Club competed in the local churches leagues. By the following year, with the assistance of Glasgow Corporation and the good offices of the Ladies Auxiliary, a Lunch Club provided a once weekly 4 course meal to deaf pensioners for a nominal charge. Again the Society had enjoyed good publicity due to the broadcasts from the church of an evening service and a

Christmas Night service in which Stewart Lochrie told the Christmas story - all this served as a reminder that:- 'the Society was formed, not by philanthropists, nor by a society of friends, but the meeting together of a few deaf people to worship.'

The public response to the 2 broadcasts was 'astonishing'. By 1966 a 'News for the Deaf' programme had been initiated by the B.B.C. Further developments in broadcasting to the Deaf saw the Society proud to be the hosts of the first Deaf Service to be broadcast on Eurovision in 1967. Later the Rev. Stewart Lochrie was to become a regular on 'Late Call' on S.T.V. and by 1972 the B.B.C. had devoted a quarterly programme 'For the Deaf' to Deaf issues. This was also the era of 'Vision On', fondly remembers by a generation of Deaf and Hearing children, many of whom cherished the ambition to win a place on 'The Gallery' for one of their artistic masterpieces.

The amalgamation with Paisley Mission paved the way for further amalgamation in 1964 with the Greenock and District Mission. As with Paisley, the Greenock Mission operated under its local committee. However administration was carried out by the Glasgow minister and secretary Stewart Lochrie. The result of this amalgamation meant that the Society now covered the whole of the West of Scotland. Plans were quickly devised for modernisation and refurbishment of all 4 institutes in Glasgow, Hamilton, Paisley and Greenock.

Continuing their strong focus on the needs of the elderly deaf, the Directors, concerned at the long waiting list of elderly people awaiting placement at Craigholme, and the lack of provision for married couples, drew up ambitious plans for another extension at a potential cost of £40,000. Yet another extension fund was launched. It was given an initial boost by a T.V. appeal by Stewart Lochrie.

The Society at this time was still engaged in the perennial battle to influence public perception of the handicap. Paradoxically the struggle had become more difficult due to the advent of the National Health Service, as has been mentioned, as well as recent technological advances. This was the era of virtually unquestioning belief in the 'White Heat of Technology' and similar false gods.

The 1965 Report states in exasperated tones:-

'How often do we hear someone remark, 'It's wonderful what can be done for the Deaf today,' and both the public and those in authority are often lulled into a sense of complacency that all is well; that in this age of astonishing technological progress, the Deaf are not being left behind. That modern hearing aids, speech training, lip reading and the Welfare State have diminished deafness as a handicap to the point of being merely a nuisance! How misinformed we are - how long must the handicapped deaf person suffer before we wake up and realise that we are no nearer to a positive solution of the dreadful handicap than we were 200 years ago.

The blunt facts are that more than 50% of deaf school leavers have very poor speech, which is either unintelligible, or is understood only by a few friends. That barely 2% of deaf school leavers attain acceptable educational standards, so that many deaf children are only semi-literate, their language severely limited, their social and economic prospects far short of their hearing brothers and sisters. This is the reality and those who would minimise this problem are doing deaf people a grave mis-service.'

The Report proceeds to make a very strong pitch for the continued necessity of Deaf Welfare workers, drawing attention to the 3 main areas of difficulty experienced by the Deaf:-

  a) Difficulties in communication which restrain the Deaf from using services even when aware they exist.
  b) Limited education which leads to shortcomings in reading and writing.
  c) The need for someone to explain and interpret for the Deaf in many situations where 'normal' people would experience no difficulty at all.

There were however some encouraging signs:- the following year the Minister for Science and Education appointed a Working Party to consider the place if any of finger spelling and signing in the education of deaf children. The Secretary of State for Scotland had also appointed a parallel Working Party to consider the nature of the guidance offered to Education Authorities in *'ascertaining children, who because of defects in hearing, are in need of special educational treatment.'*

The Society had presented submissions to both these committees, and by 1966 it had 5 fully qualified Welfare Officers for the deaf on its Staff.

Despite the extensive renovation and other financial commitments, in 1966 the Society had experienced a good year financially, showing only a small deficit. On the debit side the Society and in particular the Ladies Auxiliary had suffered a great loss with the death of Miss M.V. Johnstone, then Vice President of the Society. She had been a teacher of the Deaf for over 50 years, a member of the Auxiliary for 30 years, and 11 years a Director.

The Ladies Auxiliary itself was still thriving, running a Woman's Afternoon Guild and Evening Club - enjoying such social occasions as coloured cine shows, talks from Alcoholics Anonymous, 'Take your Pick', an Easter Bonnet Parade, visits to factories, the annual visit to the Kelvin Hall Circus, the annual Burns Supper, a Summer outing to Leven and the new Forth Road Bridge, and the annual Christmas Dinner with special guest the unforgettable Bill Tennant of S.T.V.

Services to the general Deaf Community remained:- extensive visitation was still maintained by Nurse Steen and members of the Committee; the Lunch Club was popular, a Flower Fund for the church was in place, as were the Dorcas Society and the Coal Fund. In the generally more affluent late 60's, it was noted that demand for clothing from the Dorcas Society was falling off, and due to the Clean Air Act, much more care had to be taken in providing the right fuel for the area.

The satisfaction of the Society was increased when in 1968 the Rev Stewart Lochrie received deserved recognition of his sterling services by being awarded the M.B.E.

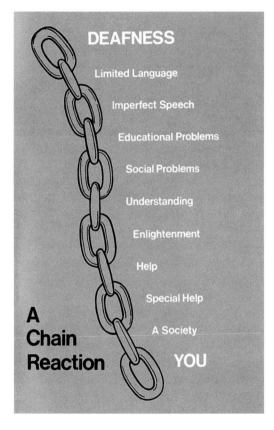

Cover 1968 Report

CHAPTER 9

THE WIND OF CHANGE

In 1969, the Wind of Change was certainly in the air for the Society. There was much contemporary discussion about Social Change - this was the era of the 'Permissive Society' and Women's Lib. If anything concern for the rapidity of change caused by advances in Technology was ever greater: partly responsible for the rise of the embryonic Green movement and the 'Hippie' subculture.

The dilemma for Humankind, as some were now realising, was that Technology seemed to be very much a double edged sword: one side bringing hope and potential prosperity, the other bringing the djinns of fear and insecurity.

The Social Work (Scotland) Act had been passed in 1969, combining all aspects of Welfare and Social Work in one comprehensive department. Should the Society 'grasp firmly the opportunities presented or opt out of Evolution by condemning it.' Here, as was the near universal contemporary view, Change was seen as Progress or Evolution. It did not seem to occur to most people of the day that there may have been a 'Third Way' in the perception of Change.

The Society was in no doubt that Evolution was a 'continuing process for good': drawing attention to the fact that 200 years before deaf people were regarded as imbeciles, with no rights under the Law. Therefore the new Act was welcomed, though it was stressed that the system whereby the Society and other voluntary organisations had acted as agents for Local Authorities was working well: though the task was daunting in that the Society was responsible for the welfare of the Deaf in an area covered at that time by 16 Local Authorities and by 7 Deaf Schools. However the Society looked on the change as an 'improvement opportunity' to strengthen services and techniques.

Steering before this 'Wind of Change', the Society decided on 18th November 1969 to change its name from 'Mission to the Adult Deaf and Dumb for Glasgow and the West of Scotland' to 'Glasgow and West of Scotland Society for the Deaf.'

The name change certainly imbued a more modern image to the Society, and implied some major differences in emphasis. First the term 'Mission' was removed and replaced by 'Society': an important change in tone.

'Mission' by the late 60's was perhaps seen as a relic of Victorian days, giving the impression of primacy of the religious dimension; perhaps also making the Society seem rather narrow and patronising in its focus - 'Society' being seen as a more encompassing modern term.

The term 'Dumb', already a term well out of fashion through linguistic connotations, not present in the 19th Century, with low intelligence, was quietly dropped, as was 'Adult'. Here the Society was taking somewhat of a risk; the term having been introduced through persistent confusion between the Society and the Deaf School, but clearly the view was that the term 'Society' should be inclusive of all sections of the Community. It is also noticeable that it is stressed in the 1969 Report that *Our churches are in fact interdenominational, though our Minister was ordained for this work by the Church of Scotland* - evidence of a more inclusive approach.

The 1970 Report was at pains to point out that the clubs then in operation:- the Lunch Club, O.A.P. (Regent) Club, Women's Guilds, Youth Club, Drama Club, Badminton, Chess and Draughts, Football, Carpet Bowls, Indoor Bowls, Camera Club and new Outdoor Club; all either competed against or had links with Hearing groups.

The major project of the time remained the ambitious and costly project to provide 'flatlets' for married couples at Craigholme. A Health and Safety inspection made necessary complete rewiring of the premises, emergency lighting, and a fire alarm system (red flashing lights) suitable for the Deaf. This extra work brought the projected cost of the scheme to £65,000. In spite of the considerable cost (there was still a shortfall in the fund of £10,000), it was decided to proceed. The foundations were to be laid in May '71, with building work planned to last for about a year.

The year 1972 saw the 150th Anniversary of the foundation of the Society. The Annual Report takes much satisfaction in the growth of the Society since those far off days when a small handful of deaf people met for a prayer meeting at the home of John Anderson in 1822. Now the Society served around 1,500 Deaf people over the West of Scotland, boasting one of the largest Deaf Centres in the U.K., and running a myriad of very successful clubs:- the Glasgow Deaf Dramatic Club had been frequent holders of the British Deaf Drama Shield for some years, Glasgow Deaf Athletic F.C. had won the Scottish Deaf Challenge Cup, the British Football Cup, and a European Trophy at Krefeld in Germany, the Chess Club had won the Scottish Championship, as had the Badminton Club, the Hamilton Bowling Club and the Greenock Table Tennis Club.

However this was, it was felt, an appropriate moment to consider the current state of the Deaf. Clearly, as has been mentioned, much had improved since 1822. The key to that improvement had been Education. But, frustrating all efforts at further improvement, it was believed, was the persistent dependence on Oralism in schools. The 1967 Government Committee had at that time come to no firm conclusions, so the Report makes a strong plea for the use of 'Total Communication', better known as the 'Combined Method' i.e. speech, lip reading, finger spelling and manual signs, as well as usable hearing; as advocated by the Gallaudet College in Washington U.S.A. with a high degree of success.

'It is interesting to note that Total Communication, or the Combined Method, is not used in our schools today, and in fact manual communication is in fact for the most part strictly prohibited. This means that education of the deaf child in this country is tied to one system, namely that of Oralism. There can be no doubt at all that a child who succeeds in this system, a child who benefits from attaining a high degree of ability in lip reading and speech, will find it less difficult to communicate in hearing society.

We are concerned, however, for the child who does not succeed in the techniques of this difficult art, the child whose ability to lipread is poor and whose speech is not easily recognisable or understood by the general public. Must we continue to deprive them of some alternative vehicle of communication? The time has surely come for more rethinking of this very real problem of how we, as a caring community, can help deaf children to overcome the tremendous problem of being unable to hear.'

Perhaps the problem was best summed up in a poem written by one of the Professors of English in the Gallaudet College:-

> *'What is it like to be curious*
> *To thirst for knowledge you can call your own*
> *With an inner desire that's set on fire -*
> *And ask a brother, sister or friend*
> *Who looks in answer and says 'Never mind'*
> *You have to be deaf to understand.*
>
> *What is it like to be laughed in the face*
> *When you try to repeat what is said:*
> *Just to be sure that you've understood*
> *And find that the words were misread -*
> *And you want to cry out, 'Please help me friend!'*
> *You have to be deaf to understand.*
>
> *What is it like to be deaf and alone*
> *In the company of those who can hear*
> *And you only guess as you go along*
> *For no one is there with a helping hand*
> *As you try to keep up with words and the song?*
> *You have to be deaf to understand.*

What is it like to comprehend
Some nimble fingers that paint the scene
And make you smile and feel serene
With the spoken work of the moving hand
That makes you part of the world at large?
You have to be deaf to understand.'

The full implications of the deprivation caused by deafness had recently been defined by Dr Eric Greenaway, the former headmaster of the Doncaster School for the Deaf as; *'Emotional frustration, moral and spiritual starvation, economic limitation and aesthetic impoverishment.'*

In spite of submissions and lobbying from Deaf societies, this perennial conflict was to continue. The Society at this point was also lobbying hard for some sort of concessionary fares scheme for the Deaf. Travel costs were spiralling, and many members lived at some distance from the Centres.

Perhaps the most fitting achievement to mark the 150th Anniversary of the Society was the opening of the new extension at Craigholme on the 15th of December 1972 by Princess Alexandra, who *'endeared herself to all members of our family at Craigholme by her simply charm and obvious warm hearted manner.'*

Princess Alexandra shares a joke with the Rev Stewart Lochrie.
The Opening of the new Extension, Craigholme.

99

To crown the 150th Anniversary year, the city of Glasgow bestowed a Civic Reception on the Society, with 600 guests invited.

1974 saw great blows to the Society in the deaths of James Montgomerie, Chairman of the Directors for 14 years, Edith Henderson a Board member for 25 years, and John Stewart the Honorary Treasurer.

However there was one encouraging development.

The Committee studying Deaf Education had published a report and booklet 'An Appraisal of Deaf Education'. A key paragraph stated that the education system in Deaf Schools should be tailored to suit the child.

Perhaps this was the first crack in the bastion of Pure Oralism. The use of 'Total Communication' in U.S.A. had spread considerably, with a good deal of success. The philosophy had now been encouraged to parents of deaf children. Many had been given instruction on the manual system and encouragement to use this with their children as well as lip reading and the use of hearing aids.

This seemed to be a hopeful development for the future, but for the Society, all was not sweetness and light.

As the 1976 Report states: *'Like all other voluntary organisations, this Society is passing through one of the most difficult periods of our existence. With the re-organisation of Local Government and the present economic climate we have yet to sail through some stormy weather.'*

The climate of social and political change was rapidly accelerating. From a present day perspective it seems that the treadmill has never stopped since: 'Change for the sake of Change' and 'Chaos out of Order' being the philosophy.

With Local Government reorganisation, the Society found itself refighting some recent battles: the main one being (yet again) striving to convince the new Regional Social Work departments of the seriousness of the handicap. But possibly the most pressing problem was a consequence of the economic and political crises of the time:- the problem of High Inflation.

This was the era of the Oil Crisis, the Three Day Week, the Miners' Strike and 'Who Rules the Country?' The unprecedented inflation rate (at one point exceeding 30%) had a catastrophic effect on the finances of the Society and all other voluntary organisations; reducing the value of grants and general funds. There is much reference to 'holding back new avenues of work' and 'stringent economies'.

The next decade was to prove one of the most difficult periods in the Society's history.

Paradoxically for the Deaf in general, there were some encouraging developments. The use of Total Communication had spread across America, had reached Europe, and was now lapping at the feet of Deaf Education in Scotland. By 1979 some schools in Scotland had made tentative steps in its introduction.

One of the factors influencing the diffusion of Total Communication was the pioneering linguistic research carried on by Bill Stokes in the U.S.A., and by others in Scandinavia. It was realised that Signing met all the necessary criteria to be termed a language since it illustrated all the linguistic forms of languages. Hence Signing gained a new respectability, at least in academic circles.

Access to World news, political developments and entertainment had been much enhanced by the introduction of 'Teletext' subtitles and the inclusion by S.T.V. of an interpreter for the Deaf in their 'Scotland Today' tea time news bulletin.

For members of the Society, there had been a most surprising new addition to the facilities at the Royal Institute: a bar! Perhaps above all else, this illustrates how social attitudes had changed. The thought of such a thing even 20 years before would have been unthinkable, but with the demise of the Temperance Society in the 50's, and the general view that liberalisation of Drinking Laws in Scotland might actually improve the situation with regard to alcohol abuse, made change more likely. One can imagine the heated debate over this issue: provision of alcoholic drinks was flying in the face of over 100 years of past tradition.

Perhaps the crucial deciding factor was the acceptance of the reality that total Prohibition rarely works. Besides it was no secret that many of the Deaf who attended the various clubs and functions at the Institute met beforehand for a drink (or two) at their unofficial meeting place at the 'Cockburn', close by to the Institute. Just as in days of yore when facilities for the Deaf were severely limited, many deaf people (especially Catholic Deaf) met to socialise, as did many migrants from the North, under the Hielanman's Umbrella in Argyle Street. The Cockburn, therefore, fulfilled a need for another type of socialisation. This need had already been partially addressed by the provision of special licences for dances and discos, but this had only increased demand for a permanent facility. The catalyst for the final change however was a most surprising benefactor: the owner of the Cockburn! The deaf customers had been one of the great institutions of the Cockburn; so much so that the owner commissioned a mural, depicting amongst others a goodly number of his deaf 'regulars'. So grateful was he for the income generated by his deaf customers, that on his death he left a generous legacy specifically for the purpose of setting up a bar in the Institute.

Ultimately, it was decided not to look a gift horse in the mouth; perhaps there was an element of 'the Devil you know', but doubtless the final clincher was the potential for the bar to be a 'nice little earner' in those days of financial difficulty. Changed days indeed.

CHAPTER 10

AN UNEXPECTED JOURNEY

Since the reorganisation of Local Government there had been great uncertainty over the position of the Society. The role of the Society as agents of the Local Authority (since the National Assistance Act of 1948) was now an uneasy one, party exacerbated by the withdrawal of Ayr Mission from a similar arrangement in the 70's. Strathclyde Regional Council had consequently appointed its first Social Worker for the Deaf. Was this the thin end of the wedge, making a direct service inevitable? What would the consequences be for the Society?

The Rev. Stewart Lochrie and the Directors had, over the years, built up a good network of communication with the Regional Social Work Department, and were able to keep arrangements to the status quo. But they were running against the tide. With the sudden death of Stewart Lochrie in January 1982, the tide became an irresistible force.

It was the end of an era for the Society. Stewart Lochrie was to be the last of the great line of Missioners: 'Father Figures' looking after all aspects of Deaf Welfare. The structure of the Society was about to be changed completely. Immediately prior to the death of Stewart Lochrie, S.R.C. had decided that there should indeed be a Direct Social Work Service for the Deaf, and negotiations over the future role of the Society, if indeed there was to be a role, were under way.

By 1983 the broad thrust of the changes had been agreed, but many problems remained. After the death of Stewart Lochrie, the Directors decided to appoint a Principal Officer, Gordon Chapman, (later the post was to be termed Chief Executive). The new Minister was the Rev H.B. Haney. The Regional Social Work Department agreed to bear the cost of the salaies of the Principal Officer and the Minister, and to pay for the use of the Society's premises at Glasgow, Hamilton and Paisley by Social Work staff. The changes in the role and structure of the Society caused major problems. As the 1983 Report states: *'The Society has gone through what is probably one of its most challenging and difficult years since it was founded.'*

Gordon Chapman, who took up his post in January 1983 was faced with an array of difficulties. Firstly there were difficulties inherent in the perception of his own role. He was not intended to act as Missionary/Secretary, responsible for every aspect of Deaf Welfare. This, in an increasingly more complex (and bureaucratic) World was seen as no longer tenable (it was suspected in some quarters that overwork may have contributed to Stewart Lochrie's untimely death). Some members, used to a 'Father Figure' found this initially difficult to accept. With the approval of the Directors, it was his function to modernise the structure of the Society. Inevitably this challenged some time honoured ways of doing things, particularly with regard to the Management Committee, and this caused more than a few ruffled feathers.

The other main area of difficulty for the Principal Officer, and the Society in general, was due to the consequences of the new Direct Service. The Society's Social Work staff, with the exception of the Principal Officer, the Minister and Mrs Margo Currie, the newly appointed Development Officer, had been transferred to the Regional Social Work staff. Most of the staff were initially unhappy with this arrangement; but there did not seem to be any choice: the Society had to 'play ball' or simply cease to exist.

The arrangement led to the extremely awkward and absurd situation that the bulk of the staff were not now directly answerable to Gordon Chapman, but to the Assistant Principal Officer of Deaf Services at Strathclyde Region.

There was particular staff unrest at Craigholme, which was experiencing extreme financial problems (possibly party due to the ambitious extension of the 70's). At any rate, staff morale was at rock bottom due to what they saw as the extremely low pay and poor conditions imposed by the Region. A Strike was threatened. At this point Craigholme was on the verge of 'going under'. Gordon Chapman however managed with difficulty to avert this, by renegotiating staff pay and conditions with the Region.

Other difficulties were caused by the general decrease in Society's staff, making coverage of the Society Centres much more difficult. This necessitated that the members of the various clubs took even more responsibility in running their own affairs.

At this stage the relationship between the Society and the Regional Social Work Department was still evolving, but there was no doubt that the priority for the Society was survival pure and simple, and the only way to ensure that survival was through full cooperation with the Region.

Partnership offered tantalising scope for future development in new areas such as running courses in Deaf Awareness and Signing. It was felt that it would be most prudent to proceed carefully down these new avenues - carefully planning a few pilot schemes rather than attempting to satisfy everyone quickly.

In order to help ordinary deaf people steer a course through the minefield caused by the changes in Social Work responsibilities, the Glasgow Management Committee set up a 'Watchdog Committee' to advise members and also to investigate any complaints about the workings of the new Direct Service.

The spiritual aspect of the work of the Society was not immune to the changes. During the all encompassing review of the services of the Society, it was realised that within the Society, and over Scotland as a whole, the Ministry for the Deaf was dangerously stretched: with only 3 Chaplains in the whole country and no replacements in the pipeline.

It was decided to approach the Kirk with the request that the John Ross Memorial Church be accepted into the Congregation of the Church of Scotland. This would mean that representatives of the John Ross could become involved in Kirk affairs, and the Kirk could provide support for the Minister and Elders.

This 'Partnership' arrangement was approved in 1983, with the responsibility for the provision of a minister and the upkeep of the John Ross being retained by the Society, and by 1986, the Society had obtained the services of a Deaconess, Miss E Miller to assist the Rev Haney in his pastoral work.

By 1984 the worst of the difficulties over the new arrangements seemed to be over, and much agonising had resulted in visions of the way forward for the Society:-

'The old image of the Charity passing round the begging bowl is diminishing rapidly and instead the Society must be seen to be providing a special professional service which meets and fills the gaps in our statutory services. The old image of the deaf person being a poor, helpless person is also diminishing, and the Society must be at the front providing the image that deaf people are capable of carrying out many tasks but need an equal opportunity . . . . . . we have come to the conclusion that in order to help deaf people achieve more equality in society, then education rather than welfare is the answer.'
(1986 Report)

Not for the first time, education was to be the panacea. The education envisaged was not only for the Deaf themselves, but also for the public as a whole. An initiative towards this 'equal opportunity' for the Deaf had already been successfully launched in the form of a computer familiarisation course with the aid of an interpreter at a local college.

Education for the public was to take the form of Deaf Awareness courses, run by the Society and now very much in demand by schools, Local Authorities, Industry and Commerce. There was now a much more general acceptance of British Sign Language (B.S.L.) as a language in its own right. Here was an opportunity for members or staff of the Society to teach sign language courses: necessitating that they themselves should be appropriately trained to deliver them.

Now that there was a Direct Service, the Society also gained some spin off benefits through better awareness of some of the Region's other services. The Community Education Department had assisted in providing trained leaders for Youth Clubs and Unemployed Clubs. The current Recession meant that there were several initiatives to improve the plight of the Unemployed.

The Unemployed Voluntary Action Group funded the training of deaf and hearing volunteers.

In the field of Deaf Education, Total Communication was making firm inroads. In the late 70's it had gradually been accepted as 'having a role for oral failures': i.e. it was still regarded as inferior to purely oral methods. Part of the problem was that some teacher training colleges and national organisations, such as the National Deaf Children's Society were still 'bastions of Oralism'. In spite of this by the mid 80's, a more flexible approach was gaining ground, aided by the general raising of the status of B.S.L.

However this process was made less straightforward by the introduction of the new educational Philosophy of Integration; reviving old arguments of Integration v Isolation. Everywhere special schools for the Deaf and other Disabled groups were starting to be closed and children with disabilities integrated either into mainstream schools or into special units attached to mainstream schools.

In terms of public awareness and understanding of disability, this philosophy had much to commend it; but for some of the Disabled Community, particularly the Deaf, this approach did not always work well, enhancing the feeling of isolation and 'being different'. Though advances in hearing aid technology had helped, few, if any children in mainstream could converse in B.S.L., and few mainstream teachers could sign. Therefore unconsciously perhaps, Integration tended once more to flag up oral methods just at the time when Total Communication seemed to be gaining ground.

By 1986, it was evident that the Society's initiatives, particularly those targeting education, had borne fruit:- *'Our philosophy of bringing about a greater recognition and understanding of deaf people's needs through education has been so successful that at times we have been gasping for breath in attempting to meet the huge demand.'*

All the Society's Sign Language, Deaf Awareness and other specialist courses for companies now had long waiting lists. To ease matters 'Quest for a Language' a new, very intensive training course for those wishing to become sign language teachers had been instituted. Approaches had been made to the Region for the completion of the course to be made an essential qualification for those employed as sign language teachers. The Manpower Services Commission Community programme had also approved the Society's 'Thumbs up' project designed to adapt essential everyday information into a manner readily understood by deaf people.

Probably the most positive development was in winning a test case, whereby the Government agreed, after some time, to fund an interpreter to enable a young deaf woman, a member of the Society, to carry out her studies on a Youth Training Scheme. The Society, working in tandem with the British Deaf Association, had made the case that this was a logical consequence of Equal

Opportunities, and thus set a precedent which resulted in new regulations which enabled a much improved level of support for deaf students.

Another important development was the appointment by the Society of a full time trainee interpreter. This was the first such post in the country.

Also, the unrest at Craigholme had subsided. There was a new officer in charge and new professionally trained staff. Part of the problem at Craigholme had been that due to the increasing general longevity, and the attitude that older people should in general stay in their own homes for longer (which would in the not too distant future lead to the Care in the Community Act), the residents were in general frailer and had much greater needs.

From being principally a Residential Home in the past, Craigholme was now more of a Nursing Home with consequent demands on Staff. Therefore Staff required much more training. It was now being considered that perhaps Craigholme should be re-registered as a Nursing Home for the Deaf, with those residents capable of a more independent lifestyle being perhaps housed in nearby sheltered housing.

Another feather in the cap for the Society was the success of the Society's athletes in the Deaf Olympics in Los Angeles. Many of those selected won medals, and one athlete, Fiona Wilson, was so successful that she was awarded the coveted 'Glasgow Sportsperson of the Year' award.

With all these positive and successful developments it looked very much, after a long period of major difficulty, that the Society had re-inventing itself and could now look forward to the future with confidence. However, perhaps inevitably, there appeared an ominous thundercloud on the horizon. A rather unexpected short paragraph in the 1986 Report states:- *'In accordance with the wishes of the membership, consideration has been given to seeking suitable alternative accommodation here in Glasgow.'*

This seems on the face of it to be very surprising. There was no mention in previous years of the unsuitability of the Institute, or indeed of any great demand amongst members for larger accommodation. Contrast this with the long 20 year campaign in the 1870's and 80's towards the lodestar of the new Institute, during which there was constant reference to the unsuitability of the current accommodation. How had this situation arisen? Was the need for new accommodation really propelled by the demands of the membership?

In fact the crux of the problem could be summed up in 2 words:- DRY ROT. It had been discovered that the building was absolutely riddled, allied with other problems such as the constant flooding of the basement. The Institute needed urgent structural repairs.

One can well imagine the expressions on the faces of the Board of Directors and other Society officials when the potential cost was revealed. It was prohibitive. With the slender funds at its disposal, just having emerged from one of the worst periods in the Society's history, the cost was impossible to bear; yet staying in the Institute was not an option; the place would probably have been falling around their ears in a year or two. Besides, it was pointed out that even in the highly unlikely event of the necessary funds being raised, the Institute was a listed building, and hence alterations to modernise the building or expand it would thus be hampered.

The blunt and highly unpalatable fact was that the Society had to move to survive.

CHAPTER 11

AN ICON CALLS

It is somewhat unclear as to whether the full extent of the structural problems at the Institute were revealed to the ordinary members or whether the potential move was presented as an opportunity to expand and modernise the Society's facilities. Perhaps in some quarters there was a wish to avoid having the finger of blame pointed in their direction for what might be seen as failure to detect and deal with the structural problems much earlier.

There were, of course, very positive aspects to the move. It was indeed an opportunity to expand, and the Institute, riddled by dry rot or not, occupied a prime site in the business quarter of the City, where office space was at a premium, and its sale thus afforded the potential of raising a very tidy sum. The sale though, by implication, would have to include the John Ross Memorial Church, and therefore any potential new property would have to include provision for a church for the Deaf. However there was no time to agonise over the move, and urgent feasibility studies of several sites were undertaken.

One site, somewhat farcically offered by the Council for serious consideration by the Society, revealed at best a somewhat patronising attitude and at worst revealed the extent of the deep seated ignorance of the needs of the Deaf. The site in question was the notorious 'Bridge to Nowhere' over the M8 Motorway at Charing Cross; the logic being that the Deaf wouldn't notice the constant traffic noise anyway! This conveniently ignored the effect of constant vibration, the potential havoc that could be caused to hearing aids by background noise, the effect on those with partial hearing, the hearing workers of the Society and the potential disruption to Deaf Awareness classes. Needless to say the proposal was summarily rejected.

However there was an unexpected twist to this saga. In the end, the feasibility study determined that it was in fact a practical proposition to erect a suitably sound proofed building above the 'Bridge to Nowhere', and accordingly an office block was erected. Therefore indirectly one can say that the Society are to blame for inflicting one of the most hideous examples of modern development on Glasgow - near the top of most Architecture lovers list of buildings in Glasgow they would most like to see blown up (the button being pressed by Prince Charles no doubt). Other sites also were rejected, and it seemed that time was running out whilst the beams of the Institute inexorably turned to dust.

Then to their credit, Glasgow District Council came up with a more realistic and creative option. They proposed that the Gorbals Library in Norfolk Street, which was due for closure, and which due to its location slightly outside the prime business district was perhaps slightly less saleable, should be exchanged for the John Ross Memorial Church and a relatively small sum of money. The only proviso to the transfer/sale being that the Society could not 'sell on' the property within 10 years. As for the Institute, the Society could dispose of it, and with the funds raised refurbish the Library to meet the needs of the Society.

The Gorbals Library was a large, structurally sound building, with great potential for modernisation and provision of new facilities. After a programme of extensive visitation, by the end of 1987 the members decided to approve the proposal. By 1988, the deal had full District Council approval and refurbishment was beginning. The architects were the well known firm of Cunningham, Glass and Murray. Gordon Murray, the main architect involved was later to be shortlisted in the design competition for the Scottish Parliament.

The Society's plans for the new building were ambitious. It was to be the largest Centre for the Deaf in the whole country. The desire was to break the mould of Deaf Centres being akin to Working Men's Clubs for the Deaf. Instead the modern facilities offered would be unsurpassed elsewhere. There were to be squash courts, an indoor bowling rink, a gym, saunas and other facilities, and last but not least, an integral church for the Deaf, retaining the title of the John Ross Memorial Church. By early 1990 the refurbishment of the old Gorbals Library was complete and the move from the Institute was under way. The move proceeded reasonably smoothly and by early summer the new Glasgow Centre for the Deaf was ready for its official opening.

The new H.Q. was to be opened by the Princess of Wales, that tragic icon of the 80's and 90's. At that time, the Princess, already semi-estranged from Prince Charles, attracted more publicity and public interest both welcome and unwelcome, than possibly anyone else on the planet. The Society could not have wished for a higher profile launch to this new era of its existence. The downside of having such a famous person was the very considerable degree of preparation required and the need for extremely tight security precautions.

In fact, securing the Princess of Wales to open the new Centre had been a long and convoluted process. The Princess's Private Secretary at Buckingham Palace had first been contacted with the request to open the new Centre by Lady Gray, the Hon. President in October 1989. The Lord Provost of Glasgow, Susan Baird had also written a letter supportive of the invitation, therefore the Society was fairly confident of a positive response. The projected opening date at that time was Spring or early Summer 1990. The Palace replied that the request would be considered at the planning meeting for the Princess's forthcoming programme to be held that December. But by the early months of 1990, the silence from the Palace was deafening. Spring arrived, then Summer: no word. No doubt the Society was well aware of the stormy personal life of the Princess at that time: indeed they probably would have to have spent the previous few years in some far off Galaxy had they not been. Perhaps this explains who no approach to the Palace was made before July. There was, before this approach, some serious consideration of abandoning the whole process. However, the Board, the Chairman Alex Nairne, and in particular Lady Gray and Alex Harrison the Head of Admin, decided on one last attempt.

Alex Harrison decided to telephone personally the Princess's new Asst Private Secretary, Commander Patrick Jephson (at the time of writing accused of disloyalty to the memory of the Princess after publishing a memoir of his time in her service), to ascertain the position. In fact, due to an oversight by his predecessor, the Society's original request had not in fact been submitted at the December planning meeting. The Commander was profuse in his apology, but when dealing with Royalty, wheels turned slowly, and he stated that the request would be submitted at the next planning meeting which, regrettably, was not until October. He did, however, thank the Society for their patience.

Frustrated by the delay, the Society decided to 'hang in there'; heir hope being that their perseverance would be rewarded: especially since it was an error at the Palace that had delayed matters for so long. In fact, the error may have been the crucial deciding factor, as, following the October planning meeting, it was announced that the Princess would have great pleasure in opening the new Centre on 20th February 1991.

Now all was frantic activity: meetings, correspondence and general liaison with Palace, the Lord Provost's Office, the Scottish Office, the Police and the Royal Protection Team. Not least a programme for the visit and a full and detailed Guest List (no easy task!) had to be drawn up, as well as a briefing for the Princess herself. One can well image the behind the scenes deliberations, agonising, rows, the 'was this really a good idea' recriminations and general mayhem. However, in a relatively short time a programme had been drawn up and a commemorative plaque ordered.

Security precautions were to be exhaustive. There was justified fear of Terrorism, the not inconsiderable number of random crackpots who took an obsessive interest in the Princess, and of course the all invasive paparazzi.

The premises had to be initially inspected by Commander Jephson and the Royal Protection Officer, accompanied by Police and representatives of the Lord Provost, to determine possible weak points in security. The building and all invited guests were to be thoroughly searched a few hours before the visit. The Press in attendance were of course to be strictly regulated.

No doubt certain elements of Gorbals Police looked forward to the opportunity of being 'High profile Polis', dramatically poised on the roof of the building: it certainly made a change from the usual drunks and junkies. Large expanses of windows facing the high flats opposite engendered fear of

Security Measures, Royal Visit.

fanatical snipers. The only acceptable solution was for the Society to order (at great expense) blinds to provide full coverage of the window area. Naturally the blinds were to be closed during the visit.

At last the great day came. No doubt the Princess was unaware of a last minute, behind the scenes security scare, caused not by terrorist activity, but by a rather more mundane activity.

Much angst, as ever on these occasions, had been generated by the vexed question as to whether the Princess might need to 'spend a penny'. Accordingly, a suitable Ladies toilet was identified and spruced up (no doubt the Princess, like the Queen, thought that the ubiquitous smell of fresh paint was completely the norm). Naturally on the day of the visit the Security team had to inspect it and the rest of the building exhaustively.

After the search the Ladies toilet was strictly out of bounds to all guests. However, just as the Princess's arrival was imminent, one nameless lady guest, unable to resist the call of nature any longer, defeated the best efforts of the Special Branch and the Gorbals Polis by penetrating the security net round the Royal toilet. A shamefaced Security Team had to mount a frantic last minute search of the toilet, complete with sniffer dogs, for offending terrorist material.

The visit lasted for 50 minutes. The Princess was introduced to Society officials and escorted on her visit by William Wilson, Chairman of the Glasgow Committee, and by Karen Fraser the head of the Interpreting Service. She toured the Administration Office, where she was introduced to Gordon Chapman and Staff, then she was treated to short performances in the Theatre by the John Ross Memorial Choir and the Canny Man Signers. In the Badminton Hall she witnessed, and participated in a 'Quest' signing class, and watched a badminton coaching class taken by Fiona Wilson, gold medallist at the Deaf Olympics and by now twice winner of the Glasgow Sportsperson of the Year title. At this point the official Media Reps had their photocall.

The Priness of Wales converses in Sign Language.

In the Lounge, she was introduced to residents of Craigholme, and observed, and became involved in a game of bowls. Thence it was to the Front Reception where the official opening ceremony took place and the plaque was unveiled; but not just by the Princess. About to pull the chord, she hesitated and turned smiling to one of the elderly residents of Craigholme and invited her forward to pull the chord with her. Then she departed for her next engagement, the visit being one of four carried out by her in Glasgow that day. All seemed touched by her genuine interest during the visit: probably these occasions distracted her somewhat from her rather traumatic personal life at that time.

The visit was over and now the Society could focus on its plans for the future in its new H.Q.

BUCKINGHAM PALACE

From: The Lady-in-Waiting to H.R.H. The Princess of Wales

22nd February 1991

Dear Lady Gray,

The Princess of Wales has asked me to thank you so very much indeed for helping to make her visit to the Glasgow and West of Scotland Society for the Deaf such an interesting and enjoyable occasion.

Her Royal Highness was delighted to have had an opportunity to hear of the Society's Work in Scotland and was most impressed by all that she saw. The Princess was very touched by the warmth of her reception and would be grateful if you could pass on to all concerned her sincere thanks for a most memorable visit.

Yours sincerely

Anne Beckwith-Smith

Miss Anne Beckwith-Smith

Lady Gray

CHAPTER 12

ENTERPRISE AND ENTREPRENEURISM

The 80's and early 90's saw the high water mark of the 'Enterprise Culture'. The culture of Change in Society and in Public Services had not abated, if anything it had accelerated. The Society had of course adapted in many ways: as a typical example it was now being considered that the 'Quest for a Language'programme should now be structured as a Community Business.

Now, however, the move to larger premises was seen as denoting an opportune time for another major review of the Society's Management and Services. An added impetus to this review was given by the potential effects to the Society of the imminent Community Care Act.

After much consultation, deliberation and careful review, by 1992 most of the changes were in place. The Constitution of the Society had been changed. The Society was now a 'Company limited by Guarantee', which maintained the Society's charitable status, but protected the Directors from responsibility in the event of the Society experiencing financial disaster.

The really big decision had been to move towards the position of giving ownership of the Society to Deaf people themselves. As an important step towards this the number of Deaf people on the Board of Directors was increased. Strategies were to be devised to ensure that deaf people involved in the running of the Society were given ongoing training in the necessary skills. The Mission Statement of the Society to this end had become 'Developing quality service in partnership with Deaf people' - a clear move away from 'Working for the Deaf' to 'Working in equal partnership with the Deaf'. In many ways this merely reflected the full implications of Equal Opportunity policy. To this end also, the Society had decided to pursue a policy of Positive Discrimination for posts vacant within it. In addition 3 new posts had been created - a Hard of Hearing Development Officer, a Community Development Officer and a Youth Development Officer.

The Management Review had been partly in response to recent legislation to introduce a 'market style' to the Caring Services, which also envisaged the Voluntary Sector playing an enhanced role in the increasingly 'contracted out' services.

As never before the philosophy of the 90's saw the Market Place as a battle-ground, and the Society had to adopt all the trappings of 90's Business speak. The organisation had to become 'lean and fit' and impose a culture of 'financial stringency', not only to compete, but also to safeguard itself against the worst effects of the Recession. Another key element in making the running of the organisation more efficient was the adoption of a system of Performance Appraisal for all Staff.

The Community Care Act was awaited with some trepidation. There was widespread public cynicism that 'Care in the Community' was a Philosophy of Convenience, whose prime function was to save money in order to fund tax cuts, which might improve the electoral prospects of a Government low in the polls.

The Society however supported the principle of Care in the Community, whilst retaining some doubts about funding and implementation. There was no question that it presented in certain aspects a threat, particularly to the running of Craigholme. There was real fear that demand for residential care would decrease; with all the financial implications of this. It would no longer be justified to place someone into care simply because they were elderly.

It was decided to meet this challenge that the Society would develop a specialist service in caring for the elderly Deaf with additional medical, physical and psychological needs. Providing this level of care would of course be more expensive, since the residents would be that much frailer. This change of emphasis also meant that Craigholme would have to be refurbished so that residents could all have single rooms.

However the legislation was also seen as providing opportunities for the Society to gain a firm foothold in the contracted out services to the Deaf, such as in Social Work, Interpreting and Environmental Aids. The Society, with its new specialist care in place at Craigholme was also well placed to provide Home Care, Day Care and Respite Care for elderly deaf people now living at home. By the time that these changes and new strategies for the future had been adopted, the Society was uncomfortably aware that a further major challenge lay ahead:- the proposed reorganisation of Local Government in 1996.

Gordon Chapman, now termed Chief Executive, clearly wearied at having yet again to write yet another Report of the 'We must change or die' variety, admits the scale of the Society's problems in 1996:-

'It seems to me that every time the Annual Report is written, it contains warnings of turbulent and difficult times ahead. Dire warnings are given about major changes in our operating environment, and fears expressed about major financial cuts. Perhaps some people might be forgiven if their initial reaction to this report is 'Oh, here we go again!' However this is not a case of an organisation crying 'Wolf!' once too often. Many of our fears and predictions are now becoming a reality and we face a very uncertain future ahead.'

The cause of these difficulties, as had been feared was the Reorganisation (or was it the re-Reorganisation?) of Local government in 1996.

The most obvious way in which the Society was affected was simply that where before they had dealt with Strathclyde: one large Local Authority; now they had to deal with 12; each one with differing structures, policies and initiatives. This of course meant a vast increase in the Society's administration, costly in terms of both finance and time, hence reducing funds and time available for work advancing the cause of Deaf Welfare.

Another difficulty which was developing was that rightly or wrongly the Society was seen in some quarters as a Glasgow based organisation, making it more difficult to negotiate future service contracts with some of the more far flung new local Authorities. The hope had to be that the Society's experience and skill in providing Deaf Services would overcome any Parochialism in wishing to see money spent remain within the Local Authority area.

Not for the first time, Finance was the most acute problem. The extent of the problem is revealed in a rather terse sentence in the Report of the new Chair, Liz McKinney in 1996:- *'Regrettably, the Society's premises at Hamilton and Paisley are now for sale.'* The Directors had concluded that given the large deficit of £84,000 and the potential difficulties ahead, maintaining 3 premises was untenable. Even fundraising, legacies and shrewd investments could not avoid this. Some store had to be laid in for the harsh times ahead, even if the sale might portray the Society as even more Glasgow based.

The Society still enjoyed a measure of financial protection from its service contract with the old Strathclyde Region, but this would soon run out. It was almost universally acknowledged that the new Local Authorities were under-funded: the Government having taken the opportunity to renegotiate Local Government block grants in its favour. With an Election looming, and with both main parties vying with each other in tax cutting agendas and promises of financial prudence, there seemed to be no sign of a slackening of the financial shackles regardless of the Election result.

The probable reality would be that the cash strapped new Local Authorities would inevitably seek savings in service contracts. At least the Society was well place to win contracts, due to their prudent focus on more specialist skills some years previously. The Society would simply have to be more flexible and focus on bidding for smaller contracts, whether in an urban or rural situation.

As if these problems were not enough, in 1997 it emerged that the Ministry of the John Ross Church was in danger. The Church of Scotland, themselves perennially cash strapped, were apparently resolved to withdraw their support for Ministry for the Deaf throughout Scotland. It was agreed that Aberdeen, Edinburgh and Glasgow would fight a joint campaign to oppose this.

After a very stormy meeting at 121 George Street (the H.Q. of the Kirk), the Church of Scotland was forced into a U-Turn. It would provide 3 Church of Scotland ministers to serve the entire Scottish Deaf Community, but only for a period of 5 years.

By 1998, Richard Durno, already well known within the Society, as he had been a Social Worker with S.R.C. and the Society, was appointed Minister, succeeding Jeanette Black, who had resigned the position, possibly because she wished a more secure post. His parish was to be a large one, extending from Stirling in the north to Galloway in the south. So the long tradition of Ministry to the Deaf within the Society was maintained, albeit on a somewhat precarious basis. It must be recalled after all that religion provided the initial impetus for the foundation and expansion of the Society.

It was ironic that yet again changes beyond the Society's control had such a negative effect on what had been in many ways a successful period in the Society's history.

The clubs, now more wholly run by the members themselves, in general were thriving in the new facilities. The Youth Development Project had been a resounding success; not only expanding the Youth Club, but also organising school leavers' courses, initiating Social Skills training and establishing a new Junior Youth Club. Working closely with schools, it had provided Sign Language and Deaf Awareness training for parents, and supported a Mother and Toddler Group. Its most novel venture had been to start a pilot 'Befriending' scheme, in which trained volunteers supported young deaf children. A very successful multilingual Sunday School for deaf children and their hearing brothers and sisters was also being run by the Chairperson Liz McKinney.

There was extremely high demand for the Society's Communication Service; particularly for support to deaf students in Higher Education. A programme of Sign Language training was well established at stages I, II and III as was the provision of short intensive courses. The classes were so popular that they did not have to be advertised!

The implications of yet another piece of new legislation promised for a change to be potentially advantageous to the Society. This was the Disability Discrimination Act, which would probably greatly increase demand for the already popular Deaf Awareness Training Classes provided by the Society. This Act of course had great potential in advancing the cause of the Deaf in general, raising the possibility of litigation towards those employers who could be proven to have been discriminatory to the Deaf.

By 1998, the Society's premises at Hamilton and Paisley had been sold. It was stated bluntly that they were 'Simply not viable'. Use of the buildings had lessened since the opening of Norfolk Street. Alternative premises had been rented to accommodate members, though the trend was that many young members preferred to attend the Glasgow Centre for Youth Activities.

Problems of Finance naturally still remained. As at 1998, the Society was only receiving financial support from 2 out of the 12 Councils; a global sum representing only 44% of the former grant from S.R.C. The other Councils, somewhat ominously were 'reviewing their positions'.

117

Clearly the Society was going to have to be less dependent on Local Authority direct funding. A heightened programme of funding was already in place to try to overcome the potential shortfall and a part time Fundraiser was employed, mainly to seek funds through grants and the National Lottery.

However, mainly due to the receipt of a large legacy, significant improvements to the Centre at Norfolk Street in order to make it 'the biggest and best Deaf Centre in the U.K' were in the pipeline.

Most crucially, repairs had to be made to the roof, which due to its 1930's design was found to have a tendency to leak: though the building was otherwise sound. In response to demand by members an extra lounge had been created at the expense of some of the space in the Snooker Room. The Office Space had been extensively modernised and moved downstairs, creating space for an I.T. Training Room.

As well as appointing a Manager for the Centre, there were several exciting new developments ongoing. Harnessing new Technology, the first Videophone communication service for the Deaf in Scotland had been set up. A grant from the Scottish Business Achievement Award Trust had enabled the purchase of the equipment necessary to set up a Videoconferencing Interpreting Service: again the first in Scotland. South Lanarkshire Council partly financed the running costs.

For some time within the Society there had been an awareness that the needs of the Deaf within the area's Asian Community were not being met. Accordingly in 1998, two successful Open Meetings were held for Asian Deaf people and their families. As a result groups from the Asian Deaf Community started to meet fortnightly in the Centre, and the Society successfully applied for funds to provide an Ethnic Development Worker in 1999. Some thought had also been given to the Gay Deaf Community, and by 2000, the first Gay Disco had been held. There were also moves afoot to increase cooperation with St. Vincent's Society for the Deaf.

In 1998 with the new Millennium looming, it was decided to freshen up the image of the Society by adopting a new name:- 'Deaf Connections', whilst retaining the old name in the Constitution. Deaf Connections, it was thought was shorter, punchier, and better described the new focus of the Society on being an 'enabling' organisation for the Deaf, not just in the West of Scotland, but across the Country as a whole.

CHAPTER 13

PAST, PRESENT AND FUTURE

The new Millennium duly arrived and swept over the Earth in a fiery cosmic tide of fireworks, hullabaloo and mass hysteria about the 'Millennium Bug'. But, as yet another dreich Scottish January progressed much as usual, you wondered what all the fuss had been about. Yet the year 2000 served the Society, as in many organisations, and indeed in society as a whole, as a time to look forward and back and, probably most importantly, to take stock of the present situation.

The changes within the organisation from its humble beginnings in John Anderson's house in 1822 had been truly incredible. However in many ways they reflected the cataclysmic changes within society in general: not surprisingly, much of the development of Deaf Connections mirrors that of society itself.

TECHNOLOGY

We are now, as in the late 60's in an era of obsession with new technology, though perhaps now we are more aware of some of the accompanying drawbacks.

As regards the Deaf and Hard of Hearing, there have been great improvements in hearing aid technology. Post aural aids using digital technology are much more specific to the needs of the individual than traditional aids. At the time of writing, these are beginning to become available on the Health Service. However these new models are very expensive, and with the strict budget limits currently set on the Health Trusts, one has to ask if they will become universally available to all, and if so will this be maintained? The hope here is that the technology, as in computing, will eventually become cheaper.

The new process of Cochlear Implantation is seen by many as a great advance. There is though, some debate on the issue. The drawbacks seem to be that the process is a major operation, with all its attendant financial implications. Additionally, at the present, the process seems to be most effective for those who have lost hearing through illness or accident - i.e. those who can recall speech. The patient after the operation is required to go on a course to learn how to interpret the electrical signals that will enable them to hear. At the moment it does not seem to be so appropriate for those adults who were born deaf.

We are in the early days of this technology. The group which is perceived to be potentially the greatest benefactors from this technology are profoundly deaf children below the age of 5. These children tend not to benefit much from hearing aids. The key aim is to enable these pre 5 children to gain auditory information from the Environment during the crucial period of language acquisition, and so prevent them from failing to develop speech and language. The advantages of Cochlear Implantation have been defined as 'Social Insertion'.

Many within the Deaf Community are wary of the process and its implications. They state that Sign Language is a Language in its own right, and that the Deaf Community should not necessarily conform to the norms of the Hearing Society. They fear that C.I's might prove a barrier to the acceptance of deafness by parents and Society in general: besides, the process is as yet experimental with unknown long term consequences, not only physiological and linguistic, but also psychological and social.

What research that has been done has been slightly contradictory. Some researchers have found that some children have not gained enough auditory information to develop speech and language, and since they had not been focussed on Signing, there was potential for estrangement from both Deaf and Hearing Communities. The great concern here is that once again, as was the case historically, that all the eggs are being put in the Oralist basket, ironically at a time when recognition of the rights of the Deaf Community is much greater than formerly.

There is little doubt though that many children seem to have benefited from the technology. Research seems to indicate that optimum results have been achieved by children who have been implanted at a very early age who have in place a network of top class support in the home, school/nursery and in the medical services; and who themselves display a positive attitude. Good progress has been measured by the 'normality' of the speech. It is an open question as to how many individuals in receipt of C.I's will ever achieve completely normal speech. It must be made clear however that the technology is advancing at great pace.

Perhaps the ultimate question to be considered is whether this technology could lead to the eventual eradication of deafness. The implications of this are not so straightforward as they seem.

If deafness is purely seen as a medical problem to be fixed, then the issue is straightforward. Yet there is a deeper philosophical issue here: deafness is not like smallpox. There is a living, vibrant Deaf Community - this could mean the extinction of that Community also.

However predictions of the beneficial qualities of several techniques and processes have been made before:- remember 'No electricity bills - free power for all from Nuclear Power!' Therefore it may be too early to have this debate;

but current indications are that the Deaf Community seems to be splitting into 2 broad camps: one saying. 'Why not accept us as we are, and realise that we can contribute to Society?' The other group seems to be very happy to embrace this new technology.

Another current problem is that some aspects of new technology broadly beneficial to the Deaf are slowly beginning to have an adverse effect on attendances at the Centre and in the various clubs and societies. This seems to be reflected country wide in a general slow decline in Deaf societies and football clubs etc. Subtitles have made television more watchable for the Deaf, but the main effects have been manifested due to the Communications Revolution. Textphones, Fax, E.Mail and the Internet make it easier for the Deaf to communicate with their fellows, hence reducing the necessity of attending the Centre. In order to address this problem, the Society plans to set up an Internet Café to meet the need. But due to developments in Videoconferencing and videophone, the need to attend may be further reduced. It all seems very far away from the era when many of the Deaf in Glasgow were forced to huddle under the Heilanman's Umbrella in order to socialise with their fellow Deaf.

Ironically, given the potential for future development in videophones, and as communication between deaf people all over the World may become more common, it may result in the system of British Sign Language having to fall into line with that practised in the rest of the World.

Advances in technology in general have meant some improvements in the general daily lives of the Deaf, with deaf compatible doorbells, alarm clocks, toys, educational software etc. Does this represent the rise of Deaf Consumerism?

Politically there seems to be a firm commitment to Social Inclusion, particularly within the Scottish Parliament. New legislation in general has meant an increased role for the Deaf in senior positions in the workplace. This, combined with the fact that the workplace is in general more demanding than in the past, has meant that some deaf people are less able or less willing to take on so much responsibility with regard to the Society and the various clubs, ironically at a time when the focus has been very much on giving the ownership of and responsibility for the Society as much as possible to the Deaf themselves, though the Society has taken steps to offset this problem by initiating an induction programme to introduce potentially promising people into the workings of the Society.

EDUCATION

Throughout the history of the Society, it was often stated that Education was the key to the advancement of the cause of the Deaf. Looking at the subject objectively, it must be said that in some ways Education was the key to the suppression of the Deaf.

As someone who is 'manually illiterate', with before undertaking this history only very limited knowledge of Deaf affairs, what strikes me most powerfully is how seldom anyone concerned with Deaf Welfare seems to have listened to the Deaf themselves. Nowhere is this more marked than in the field of Education.

After the infamous Conference of Milan in 1880, the deaf were subjected to a century in which their own language was virtually proscribed and the system of Pure Oralism enforced on them, at which most were preordained to fail. The white hot anger of the Deaf themselves still burns against this even now.

The motives of those who imposed this, few of whom were deaf themselves, were many and various. Harlan Lane the Deaf Historian terms this 'The mask of Benevolence'. For a full account of the suppression of Sign Language and Deaf History in general, I can do no better than to recommend his lyrical, angry history 'When the Mind Hears'.

At the time of the Conference, there was rivalry between schools, and Oralism was seen as a modern doctrine; but the crux of the matter was probably that teaching deaf people to speak was much more socially acceptable. Hearing people for the most part did not understand Sign Language, and what people do not understand they often fear, or at best do not value. As Lane states:- *'People are quite afraid of Human Diversity, and look to their social institutions to limit it or eradicate it.'*

It may be said that most of the individuals at the Conference were well meaning. Perhaps they were, but the road to Hell is often paved with good intentions. Under the 'Mask of Benevolence', no-one seems to have consulted the Deaf as to which system was most suitable to their needs. No doubt many meant well, but concern for the Deaf seems to have taken second place to self-aggrandisement and intellectual purity. Most took the view that Signing was a sort of basic code, not a proper language, and of course inferior to spoken language.

There were those deaf people who were able to benefit from the Oralist system, but they were in very much of a minority. For every Evelyn Glennie the system produced there were a host of people that the system failed.

Many still believe that L'Abbe de L'Epee invented the manual system. This is not the case: the Deaf themselves had already developed the system. Where L'Abbe de L'Epee deserves credit is that he actually listened to the Deaf themselves in allowing them to teach him signing, and thence he adapted it in order to educate them, founding the first school for the Deaf.

As has been mentioned, it is only in recent decades that Sign Language has been recognised (by some) as a language in its own right, thus paving the way for 'Total Communication' in Education. It can be argued that although the status of Sign Language has been enhanced, it still has not reached parity with Oral Language. Even now Total Communication is regarded by some as being only for 'oral failures'.

The system of Bilingualism is making some headway in certain parts of the World. In this the 2 languages are given equal parity and one language is 'grafted on' to another. The system though does not seem to have made any progress in Scotland.

Integration and Inclusion are the key words in Education today, not just for the Deaf, but also for all those children physically or mentally handicapped. Many Deaf Schools are closing or have closed. Whilst some schools retain Deaf units, many deaf children have been integrated into mainstream schools. In some ways, this is a good thing. It should enhance the understanding in Society in general of the problems of the Deaf. It will probably raise the academic standards of deaf pupils.

However the process has its down side. It requires a high level of support. Are there enough trained teachers of the Deaf to go round? Is the funding adequate? One has to ask whether peripatetic teachers of the Deaf waste valuable time in travel. As has been already touched on, there is the problem of Isolation. Many deaf children in a mainstream class may feel 'Different', lonely and cut off from their fellows. The generally oral environment may dissuade Signing. Those with poor speech may be reluctant to take part in discussion and become introverted, whilst those with good speech may conceal the extent of their hearing difficulties.

Again one wonders if the philosophy of Integration follows the agenda of those parents who regard deafness as a social stigma or those politicians who see it as a cheaper option, or whose liberal philosophy does not make them stop and ask what is best of the Deaf. It may be that Deaf Units within mainstream schools are the best model: giving a measure of Integration, whilst maintaining social contact with the Deaf Peer Group and keeping resources centralised.

There is now a strong impetus within the Deaf Community to have B.S.L. recognised as Britain's fourth official language. Intensive lobbying is taking place. The partial inclusion of B.S.L. in the 5-14 and National Curriculum is under consideration.

The Federation of Deaf People

BSL MARCH 2000

British Sign Language is the first or preferred language of 70,000 people. It needs to be recognised by the Government as Britain's fourth official language!

8th JULY 2000

Meet: 11am SHARP for a 12 noon start.
At Temple Place, London WC2

Tube: Temple (or Embankment/Blackfriars)
Coaches drop off on Victoria Embankment next to Temple Tube Station.

Rally at Trafalgar Square on Arrival!

BE THERE!

Petitions

BOOK YOUR COACHES NOW!

Fundraising

EVEN BIGGER AND BETTER!

More Information: BSL March 2000, FDP, PO Box 11, Darwen, Lancashire BB3 3GH.
Fax: 01254 708071   Email: bslmarch@aol.com

A recent Rally as part of the Campaign to get B.S.L recognised as Britain's 4th Official Language.

WHY UHURA WEARS A SHORT SKIRT; VISIONS OF THE FUTURE

Divination of the Future has always been one of Humankind's obsessions. Generally it is a mug's game. The only thing that can probably be said about the Future for the Society and the Deaf in general is that probably for the most part it won't be what we expect.

The Future, for too many Futurologists and Star Gazers, is really too often seen in terms of the Present. Look from our position of hindsight back to those 1950's Science Fiction movies, or the 60's Star Trek episodes. They turned out to be, well, pretty much about the 50's and 60's and the current themes and issues of those days. If we examine great movies of the 20's and 30's such as 'Things to Come' or 'Metropolis', we see much the same thing: obsession with the rise of Totalitarianism and Social Conflict, contrasted with post World War I Utopias: reflecting the hopes and fears of Society of the day. It is of course true that some authors and directors used the Future wholly or partly as a device to make social comment on their contemporary Society.

Paradoxically, theories of the Past have also been seen in terms of the Present, reflecting the current in-doctrines and preoccupations of the era.

Archaeological theories and interpretations of the Past of the 30's reflected views on Racial Conquest, struggles of the Masses and 'Lebensraum' type movements of peoples. Those of the 60's reflected obsessions with technology and covert organisations:- The Megalithic Yard, Priest Astronomer Castes etc. Those of the 70's and 80s were often seen in terms of Ecological disaster, whereas many current theories seem to reflect our current obsession with Sex.

It's all too easy to fall into the trap. One of the main purposes in studying History is to help understand the Present, and hence anticipate the Future. Too many people forget this. There's always a tendency to see ourselves at this moment in time as ultra modern, on the verge of a more civilised and enlightened Society. We must remember that many of our ancestors in 1870 and 1930 thought exactly the same. It's amazing how often the terms 'Modern' and other quasi Future speak, as well as, on the other hand 'outdated' and 'backward-looking' are used by those on the make.

If History does teach one thing, it is that the Past is usually repeated in the Future and the mistakes of the Past are almost invariably repeated in the Future; perhaps in a different form or context, but repeated they usually are. And in a Deaf context, the main mistake would be not to consult the Deaf as to what is best for them.

Our Society could not repeat its past repression of the Deaf, could it? Surely all that has changed and Society in general is much more Deaf aware?

Two incidents of the very recent past, recounted to me a short time ago illustrate that problems still remain. A member of the Society was en route to the Centre for the Deaf by the Glasgow Underground. At the station before his stop, everyone on his carriage left the train. Much to his surprise the train then sped past his station and several others. It then halted in a brightly lit area, and after some shunting, to his astonishment he felt the whole carriage being hoisted aloft. Terrified, he staggered over to the window and proceeded to hammer frantically. As luck would have it, he was promptly spotted by a started crane driver, who immediately lowered the carriage and released him from his swaying prison. Of course a tannoy announcement had been made that the train was being taken out of service for essential maintenance, but no-one had considered that this might not have been heard, and no proper checks had been made. The man, escorted to the surface by shamefaced workmen, fled, and was too embarrassed to complain.

An Official of the Society, whose elderly deaf mother was about to undergo a major operation, was asked by the Consultant if it was worth trying to resuscitate her in the event of problems developing, as she was, after all, profoundly deaf.

Only the constant vigilance of the Deaf and their supporters will avert future injustices, but this will not be easy. Social Justice usually plays second fiddle to the God of Money, and future threats will come from new and unanticipated directions. It is noticeable that currently, funding is being found for expensive cochlear implants more easily than for more signing teachers and interpreters.

Paradoxically, at a time when the movement for proper recognition of B.S.L. is strong, other developments such as perhaps Integration in Education, and especially technological developments may lead to conscious or unconscious opportunities to suppress the Deaf Language.

As has been discussed, technological developments may even lead eventually to the eradication of Deafness itself. Is this wholly desirable? In many ways it might seem so, but what do the Deaf themselves think? If Homosexuality was thought to be purely a medical problem, fixed by an operation, would all Gay people be willing to undergo medical treatment to make them 'normal'? Many of course are sceptical as to whether technology, and the funding for it, will ever reach a level to make any of these scenarios in any way plausible.

As for the Society, since the situation for the Deaf has improved in the workplace and socially, there may well be less demand for its facilities. There will always be the need for the Deaf to socialise, but there are now alternative ways to socialise. But then, the ultimate aim for the Society and other Deaf organisations has always been for the Deaf to be catered for and accepted by mainstream Society. In the end, it may be that the ultimate success of the Society will be realised on the day when it can shut up shop and cease to exist.

EVOLUTION OF THE NAME OF THE SOCIETY

DATE	NAME
1822 - 1872	The Scottish Association for the Deaf and Dumb, Glasgow Branch. (Sometimes also termed 'The Scottish Deaf and Dumb Association', Glasgow Branch)
1872 - 1873	The Glasgow Christian Association of Deaf and Dumb
1873 - 1889	The Glasgow Mission to the Deaf and Dumb
1889 - 1908	The Glasgow Mission for the Adult Deaf and Dumb
1908 - 1969	Mission to the Adult Deaf and Dumb for Glasgow and the West of Scotland ('Glasgow Mission to the Adult Deaf and Dumb' retained in the Constitution)
1928	Name altered in the Constitution
1969 - 1998	Glasgow and West of Scotland Society for the Deaf
1998 -	Deaf Connections ('Glasgow and West of Scotland Society for the Deaf' retained in the Constitution)

DEAF CONNECTIONS: PLACES OF WORSHIP

YEAR	LEADER	PLACE OF WORSHIP
1822 - 24	John Anderson	His own home, St Andrew's Square
1825 - 26	Mr J. Ferguson	A Medical Lecture Room, North Portland Street
1826 - 44	Very occasional Services, conducted by the members themselves	
1844 - 48	William Ure	Hall at the Andersonian University
1848 - 50	Archibald Cameron	Balfour's School, North Portland Street
1850 - 54	Occasional Services, conducted by members	
1854 - 56	Colin Campbell	Room at the Andersonian University
1857 - 59	William Curle	Y.M.C.A., North Frederick Street
1859 - 64	Occasional Services, conducted by members	
1864 - 68	Daniel Weir	Room, Andersonian University
1868 - 70	John Weir	Room, Andersonian University
1870	David Lindsay, John Heggie James Paul (Rota)	Room, Andersonian University
1870 - 73	Alex Stathern	Room, Andersonian University
1874	James Howard (1st Missionary)	Room, Andersonian University
1874 - 75	A. Frederick Woodbridge	Room, Andersonian University
1874 (25.10)	A.F. Woodbridge	Anderson Church (1st ever Communion Service wholly for the Deaf)
1875 - 78	A.F. Woodbridge	Hall, 126 Renfield Street
1878 - 83	John Henderson	Hall, 126 Renfield Street
1883 - 95	John Henderson	'Hope Hall', 65 Renfrew Street
1895 - 1928	John Henderson	Royal Institute, West Regent Street
1928 - 31	George Nicholson	Royal Institute, West Regent Street
1931 - 34	George Nicholson	John Ross Memorial Church
1934 - 49	James W. Greig	John Ross Memorial Church
1949 - 82	J. Stewart Lochrie	John Ross Memorial Church
1982 - 90	Hugh B. Haney	John Ross Memorial Church
1990 - 92	Hugh B. Haney	John Ross Memorial Church, Centre for the Deaf, Norfolk Street
1992 - 98	Janette Black	John Ross Memorial Church, Centre for the Deaf, Norfolk Street
1998 -	Richard Durno	John Ross Memorial Church, Centre for the Deaf, Norfolk Street

MISSIONARIES/MINISTERS OF THE SOCIETY

1874 (Jan - Oct)	James Howard
1874 - 78	A. Frederick Woodbridge
1878 - 1928	John Henderson
1928 - 34	George Nicholson
1934 - 49	James W. Greig
1949 - 82	J. Stewart Lochrie
1982 - 92	Hugh B. Haney
1992 - 98	Janette Black
1998 -	Richard Durno

TIME LINE

1815	Battle of Waterloo		
		1819	First school for the Deaf in Glasgow
		1822	Foundation of the Society by John Anderson
		1824 - 68	Services erratic
1837	Reign of QueenVictoria begins		
1854	Crimean War		
1862	American Civil War		
		1868	Langside School for the Deaf opens
		1871	Football Club founded
1872	Education Act	1872	1ˢᵗ Annual Report
		1874	1ˢᵗ Missionary - James Howard
1876	Custer's Last Stand	1876	Penny Savings Bank, Reading Room established
		1878	Temperance Society founded
1880	Conference of Milan		
		1883	Society moves to 'Hope Hall'
		1891	Ladies Auxiliary founded
		1895	Opening of Royal Institute
1899	Boer War		
		1900	Y.M.,Y.M.C.A. founded
1905	Russo-Japanese War		
1914	World War 1		
1916	Russian Revolution, Easter Rising		
1919	Spanish Flu pandemic		
		1925	1ˢᵗ Society Magazine
1926	General Strike		
1928	Universal Suffrage		
		1931	Opening of John Ross Church
		1932	Visit of Helen Keller, Duke & Duchess of York
1933	Hitler becomes Chancellor of Germany		
		1935	1ˢᵗ Employment Scheme
1936	Abdication of Edward VIII		
		1937	Mauldslie Scheme established
1939	World War II		
1945	V.E. and V.J. days, 1st Atom Bomb		
		1949	Opening of Craigholme
1952	Queen Elizabeth II		
1956	Suez Crises		
1957	'Sputnik' - 1st Artificial Satellite		
1961	1st Man in Space - Yuri Gagarin		
1962	Beatles 1st No 1 Single	1962	Amalgamation with Paisley Mission
		1966	B.B.C. 'News for the Deaf' established
1969	1st Moon Landing		
		1972	Craigholme Extension opened
1982	Falklands War		
1984	Miners' Strike		
		1990	Move to new H.Q. Norfolk Street
1991	Gulf War	1991	Opening of H.Q. by Princess of Wales
		1998	Name 'Deaf Connections' adopted
1999	Opening of Scottish Parliament		

There was for a time in the 1880's a tradition within the Society to include a poem at the close of the Annual Report. In the interests of continuity here's one for today.........

A Second home in the Second City

i

Nor Wester slashing the Clyde
Beggars crosslegged on the puddled bridge
Polystyrene cups in outstretched hands.
Any sperr chynge pal?
The 'Buddy can you spare a dime?' of this town.
The city soars behind,
Cranes and towered glass,
The green domes of the Second City.
Tobacco Lords and e-commerce,
Shebeens and the demon drink,
Heroin and Alcoholism,
The Orange and the Green.
What has changed?
The Gyres revolve, no escape.

ii

At the Deaf Centre cybersigning,
Text, fax and e-mail.
Air draughty with conversation,
Gossip, jokes, scandal.
'Ma Mother always called this her second Hame.'
Peel off the mask of normality.
A Second Home in the Second City.

ROBERT J. SMITH
February 2001

BIBLIOGRAPHY

ATHERTON, M; RUSSELL, D; TURNER, G.H. 2000. 'Deaf United'. COLEFORD; DOUGLAS McLEAN

BROOKS, SANDY. 2000. 'Summary History of Glasgow Deaf Athletic'. (PAMPHLET)

'The Deaf Herald', 1937 - '39

'The Deaf Scot' Magazine, ISSUES 1 - 4

DIMMOCK, A.F. 1993 'Cruel Legacy'   EDINBURGH; SCOTTISH WORKSHOP PUBLICATION
                                       DONALDSON'S COLLEGE.

LANE, HARLAN. 1984 "When the Mind Hears'. LONDON; VANTAGE

'Magazine of the Mission to the Deaf and Dumb of Glasgow and West of Scotland', 1925.

Magazine for the Scottish Deaf', 1929 - '36.

NIXON, GILLIAN. 2000   'The role of Standardised and Naturalistic Assessment when Evaluating the
                          Progress of Profoundly Deaf Children with Cochlear Implants'.
                          (UNPUBLISHED THESIS)

PENNEY, SCOT MONCRIEFF. 1919.   'Education of the Deaf and Dumb in Glasgow 1819 - 1919'.
                                   GLASGOW. JOHN HORN LTD.

SOCIETY MINUTES:-   COMMITTEE
                       DIRECTORS

SOCIETY ANNUAL REPORTS. 1871 - 1999.

SMITH, ALEXANDER. 1880. 'A Summer in Skye'. EDINBURGH. N.R. MITCHELL & CO